The Strange
Non-Death
of Neoliberalism

Colin Crouch

polity

First published in 2011 by Polity Press
Reprinted in 2012, 2013

Polity Press
65 Bridge Street
Cambridge CB2 1UR, UK

Polity Press
350 Main Street
Malden, MA 02148, USA

ISBN-13: 978-0-7456-5120-0
ISBN-13: 978-0-7456-5221-4(pb)

A catalogue record for this book is available from the British Library.

Typeset in 11 on 13 pt Sabon
by Toppan Best-set Premedia Limited
Printed and bound in the USA by Edwards Brothers, Inc.

The publisher has used its best endeavours to ensure that the URLs for external websites referred to in this book are correct and active at the time of going to press. However, the publisher has no responsibility for the websites and can make no guarantee that a site will remain live or that the content is or will remain appropriate.

Every effort has been made to trace all copyright holders, but if any have been inadvertently overlooked the publisher will be pleased to include any necessary credits in any subsequent reprint or edition.

For further information on Polity, visit our website: www.politybooks.com

The Strange
Non-Death
of Neoliberalism

for Joan

Contents

Acknowledgements

I am grateful to Joan Crouch for many years of listening to and contributing to the ideas in this book; to Mari Prichard for undertaking the hapless task of reading an earlier draft and trying to persuade me to turn social science English into something readable; to Mark Harrison for advising on one or two points of economics; to my colleagues and students in the International Centre for Governance and Public Management at the University of Warwick Business School, in teaching and otherwise working with whom I developed many of my arguments; and to Polity's three anonymous referees, who gave such kind and constructive advice for improvement of my initial draft. Since I did not necessarily take the advice of any of these and they do not necessarily agree with me, they are not responsible for anything that appears here.

Preface

The financial collapse at the turn of 2008–9 seemed to mark a major crisis for the set of economic ideas that have ruled the western world and many other parts of the globe since the late 1970s. Those ideas are generally grouped under the name 'neoliberalism'. There are many branches and brands of neoliberalism, but behind them stands one dominant theme: that free markets in which individuals maximize their material interests provide the best means for satisfying human aspirations, and that markets are in particular to be preferred over states and politics, which are at best inefficient and at worst threats to freedom.

The financial collapse challenged these ideas because it involved the world's leading banks. They are profit-maximizers, acting in the purest of markets; how can they possibly not have contributed to the sum of human welfare in all that they did? How could it be that today's financial markets, the most sophisticated form of the market probably in human history, could run into trouble of such a massive kind, when the most advanced economic theory had demonstrated that unregulated financial markets will be self-correcting? If we have been told, even by governments themselves, that government is far less efficient than firms in the market, and that the less involved government becomes in the market, the better, why did the banks go to governments for enormous sums of money to bail them out of their difficulties? And why did governments accept their arguments? Is it really true that big banks are 'too big to fail', and that governments and taxpayers must rush to help them if they get into trouble? But if that is so, are we not admitting that there are severe limits to what the market can achieve, and that neoliberalism has been found wanting in its central claims?

In 1936 George Dangerfield published a book entitled *The Strange Death of Liberal England* (London: Constable). It tried to explain the sudden collapse in the early twentieth century of the political ideas and political party that had dominated the late nineteenth century in that country. The equivalent task today is, however, *not* to explain why neoliberalism will die following its crisis, but the very opposite: how it comes about that neoliberalism is emerging from the financial collapse more politically powerful than ever. Whereas the financial crisis concerned banks and their behaviour, resolution of the crisis has been redefined in many countries as a need to cut back, once and for all, the welfare state and public spending. And the issue today is not limited to a single country, as neoliberalism is an international, even global, phenomenon. What we have to understand today is, therefore, the strange non-death of neoliberalism.

At the heart of the conundrum is the fact that actually existing, as opposed to ideologically pure, neoliberalism is nothing like as devoted to free markets as is claimed. It is, rather, devoted to the dominance of public life by the giant corporation. The confrontation between the market and the state that seems to dominate political conflict in many societies conceals the existence of this third force, which is more potent than either and transforms the workings of both. The politics of the early twenty-first century, continuing a trend started in the previous one and accentuated rather than weakened by the crisis, has become, not a confrontation at all, but a series of comfortable accommodations among all three. A central aim of this book is to show why a political debate that continues to be organized around market and state is missing the issues raised by this important phenomenon.

The political power of the corporation is seen most obviously in the extraordinary lobbying activity that takes place, primarily in the United States Congress, but also around many other legislatures and governments. It is also highly visible in the capacity of transnational firms to 'regime shop' when choosing in which parts of the world to locate their investments. But these phenomena are considerably reinforced by further factors. First is the increasing tendency of governments to subcontract delivery of many of their own activities to private firms, which then become involved in shaping public policy. Second is the growth of corporate social responsibility, a process whereby firms take on tasks going beyond conduct of their actual business, in effect again making public policy. Third is the one signalled at the outset: the way in which, far from casting doubt on the role of giant corporations, especially financial ones, in contemporary society, the financial crisis of 2008–9 has served only to reinforce their power.

I discussed some of these issues briefly in my book *Post-Democracy* (Polity, 2004), in which the power of the global corporation appeared as one of a number of factors that I saw as leading our democracy towards becoming something of an empty shell. Further developments in the factors listed above make it necessary to return to the theme, exploring further what happens to democracy and politics when many corporations become not just mighty pressures on, but major insider participants in, the political process. This is something which no economic or political theory defends or advocates in any way; but it is a central reality of our public life.

One consequence is that democracy is joined by the market as a kind of victim. This might seem surprising, as most political debate does not distinguish between the market and firms. But it is precisely in that lack of a distinction that several of our problems lie, rendering rather outmoded the confrontation between 'state and market' that occupies so much attention. One might talk of a triangular confrontation among state, market and the corporation, but I prefer 'comfortable accommodation'. This is partly because corporate power makes it its business to bind them all together, but also partly because the only alternative to some kind of accommodation would be a rather wretched society, in which at least one of the three was crippled into becoming non-functional. It needs only a little reflection to realize how difficult life would then become.

It is not therefore the purpose of this book to argue that somehow we should rid ourselves of giant corporations. The odd bedfellows of Jeffersonian liberals and Marxists who would have sought such an outcome both belong to an unrealistic past. Instead, this book looks to a fourth force, the busy but small voices of civil society, not to abolish, but to criticize, harry and expose the misdeeds and abuses of the cosy triangle. This in no way promises a different social order from corporation-dominated capitalism, but, provided our societies remain open and vigilant, it can make life far better than states and corporations will do if left to themselves.

Badly, very badly, to misquote Andrew Marvell:[1]

Thus, though we cannot make the corporation
Stand still, yet we will make him run.

[1] Andrew Marvell (1621–78) ended his poem 'To His Coy Mistress' (a very different context) with the lines:

Thus, though we cannot make our sun
Stand still, yet we will make him run.

About this Book

Most literature about subjects of this kind is written from the standpoint of someone showing how the world might be changed, either by the authors themselves if they ever got their chance, or by political leaders whom they hope to address. But very few people are ever in a position to change the world, and among those few are many who would change it for the worse. There is a far, far bigger audience of people who have to cope as best they can with the world they find. It is for them that this book is written. *Post-Democracy* originated in a pamphlet I had written for the Fabian Society, entitled *Coping with Post-Democracy*. The title was simplified for the book, but the intention was the same: how to cope with a world largely beyond the control of ordinary people. The present book is a sequel to *Post-Democracy*. It deals with some overlapping themes, and it is also addressed to those who have to cope.

Also like the earlier book, it is addressed to the general reader and is not an academic study. It does not therefore carry the important burden of references and footnotes necessary to scientific work, but just gives a few general references and ideas for further reading for each chapter.

Some of the chapters are attempts to produce more generally accessible accounts of my own academic work, in particular:

Chapters 2 and 4 draw on my chapter 'Marketization', in M. Flinders et al. (eds), *The Oxford Handbook of British Politics* (Oxford: Oxford University Press, 2009), pp. 879–95. This material is used by permission of Oxford University Press.

Chapter 3 makes use of my chapter 'The Global Firm: The Problem of the Giant Firm in Democratic Capitalism', in D. Coen (ed.), *The Oxford Handbook of Business and Government* (Oxford: Oxford University Press, 2009), pp. 148–72. This material is used by permission of Oxford University Press.

Chapter 5 is based extensively on my article 'Privatised Keynesianism: An Unacknowledged Policy Regime', *The British Journal of Politics and International Relations* 11/3 (2009): 382–99.

Chapter 6 makes some use of my article 'Modelling the Firm in its Market and Organizational Environment: Methodologies for Studying Corporate Social Responsibility', *Organization Studies* 27/10 (2007): 1533–51.

Chapter 7 makes some use of my chapter 'Privates, Publics and Values', in J. Benington and M. Moore (eds), *Public Value: Theory and Practice* (Basingstoke: Palgrave Macmillan, 2010).

1

The Previous Career of Neoliberalism

As we shall consider in more detail below, neoliberalism began its dominance when its opposed predecessor, generally known as Keynesian demand management, entered its own massive crisis in the inflation of the 1970s. If this crisis proved more or less terminal, should we not now expect the end of neoliberal dominance and the emergence of something new following its crisis? No. Keynesianism's crisis led to its collapse rather than to adjustments being made to it, not because there was something fundamentally wrong with its ideas, but because the classes in whose interests it primarily operated, the manual workers of western industrial society, were in historical decline and losing their social power. In contrast, the forces that gain most from neoliberalism – global corporations, particularly in the financial sector – maintain their importance more or less unchallenged. Although it was the behaviour of the banks that caused the 2008–9 crisis, they emerged from it more powerful than before. They were considered so important to the early twenty-first-century economy that they had to be protected from the consequences of their own folly. Most other sectors, hurt by the effects of the crisis, were not protected. The public services fared even worse, being required to take massive cuts in resources. While the very large bonuses paid to some banking staff became a central issue in the controversy following the crisis, continued payment of bonuses was then justified as being necessary to return the financial sector – and therefore whole nations – to solvency, even though those bonuses depended in part on the contributions of taxpayers to the rescue operation. The financial sector has demonstrated the dependence of the rest of society on its operations – at least in the Anglo-American world which has nurtured this particular form of banking activities. And as it has been protected while other sectors in general and public services are being cut, it will loom larger than ever in the economic structure of those countries.

Before we consider the implications of this situation for neoliberalism's claims to be about free markets, we must first take a closer look at neoliberalism itself: what is it and where did it come from? Then, in Chapters 2–4 we shall examine the standard debate of 'state versus market', and how the corporation emerges as of primary importance from that confrontation, changing its nature in the process. In Chapter 5 we return to study in more detail the shift from Keynesianism to neoliberalism mentioned above and its wider implications; this ends by demonstrating why the corporation emerges as the key institution following the recent crisis. Chapter 6 examines the political contours of societies in which corporations have acquired political centrality, including consideration of the idea of corporate social responsibility. Chapter 7 shifts the discourse and moves to a theme that darts in and out of the preceding chapters: where do values, and in particular those concerning public and collective issues, stand in the relation between market, state and corporation? The final chapter tries to provide some answers to the question: how do we cope with all this?

Neoliberalism: Its Origins and False Start

Many of the words that we today use to describe public life contain the prefixes neo-, new or post-: neoliberal, neoconservative, New Labour, postindustrial, postmodern, post-democratic. We seem determined to show that we are people busily involved in momentous systemic change, but we are not sure what new state we have entered, so we name ourselves in terms of what we are leaving behind (post- concepts) or hint vaguely at renewal and innovation (neo- concepts). Neoliberalism is one of these. To gain an initial understanding of it, we need to know what liberalism is (or was), and what is meant by the prefix.

'Liberalism' is about as slippery as a political term can be. Today it tends to move to the political left as one heads westwards. In Europe, and especially in the former state-socialist countries of central and eastern Europe, it is associated with political parties that stand for the strict application of market principles to economic life, as well as for extensive civil liberties. The former is normally associated with the political right, the latter with the left. In the USA it tends to refer to the political left in general; this shares the European commitment to civil liberties and criticism of any political power exercised by organized religion, but is diametrically opposite to this tradition when it comes to the market. American liberals are likely to believe in government intervention in the economy, the opposite of the usual and historical meaning of the term.

To understand this complexity we have to go back to the seventeenth and eighteenth centuries, when criticism of the combined powers of monarchs, aristocrats, popes and bishops was gathering pace across Europe and, later, North America. These powers did not accept that people in general had rights; only privileges and specified liberties (plural) granted and revocable by the powers themselves. While the struggle was at the level of ideas and for freedom of thought, an alternative power base to those of church and the monarchical state was available in the commercial and, eventually, industrial wealth of the bourgeois classes. The demand by merchants for markets to be freed from the control of secular and religious authorities, who enjoyed the revenues they received for granting trading monopolies, joined the general cry for liberty as a singular, indivisible quality, a human right that it was in no one's power to grant. In practice, in a world in which existing powers in church, state and land-ownership could not be simply wished out of existence, the pursuit of liberty took the form of seeking various separations: of state from economy; of church from polity; of all of these, and even of family, from moral judgements over how individuals conducted their lives. Through the compartmentalization of life that could be achieved by these separations, the reach of power could be limited and individual liberty achieved.

From the perspective of conservatives, this same process left individuals alone, anomic and without a shared morality, and society fragmented and rudderless. By the end of the nineteenth century bourgeois property-ownership and the associated liberal right to own factories and other bases of economic activity, including that to employ labour, had themselves become sources of domination and power. Workers and others, whose lives could not achieve much separation from the control of employers, now sought liberty from them too. They looked to the gradually democratizing state for counterbalancing power. Social critics also turned their opposition to the increasing dominance of commercial values and money over all areas of social life. The liberal tradition was broken in two.

On the one hand, there was a social part, which concentrated on the search for rights, including the right of the working masses to raise themselves above poverty, and which increasingly and paradoxically looked to liberals' old enemy, the state, for help in that search. These liberals often found themselves in the uncomfortable company of socialists, who wanted to use state power to suppress capitalist property-ownership. But there was also an economic part, which stressed the liberties of property-ownership and market transactions. Liberals of this kind now increasingly found themselves uniting with their old conservative enemies, protectors of the old regime, defending authority and property-ownership of all kinds from attack, particularly from democracy. A democratic state dominated by a propertyless working class threatened to oppose the separation between economy and polity that was central to both the concept of liberty and the efficient functioning of the market. In a further complication, social liberals, socialists and conservatives would sometimes come together to denounce the triumph of materialist values and absence of moral judgements that capitalism and economic liberalism had brought about. Different strands of liberalism, whether in the form of systems of thought or of political parties, went their separate ways, with different emphases in different parts of the world.

By the time of the Second World War, the whole context of liberalism's original confrontation with the state had changed. During the 1920s the liberal capitalist economy with minimal state intervention seemed to have failed and brought the world to major depression. By the 1930s three alternative approaches to the organization of economic life seemed to offer far more efficiency and capacity to thrive: the communism being practised in the USSR; the fascism of Germany and Italy; and various combinations of government demand management and welfare state initiatives being practised in the USA and the Scandinavian countries, briefly also in France. Different though they were from each other, all made use of the power of the state in a way not envisaged in classical liberalism. After the war, one of these, fascism, was (with some exceptions) crushed. The Soviet state ruled half of Europe with dictatorial powers but, as it seemed at the time, with some economic competence; it was soon to be joined, though in only uneasy and temporary political alliance, by a similar system in the world's most populous country, China. In western Europe, North America, Japan, India and Australasia highly diverse forms of the US-Franco-Scandinavian approach of varied economic and social interventions by a democratic state into a definitely capitalist economy attracted support from virtually all shades of political and intellectual opinion. It seemed that the original liberal vision of an economy governed by the market with minimal state involvement was dead. Liberalism could live on in its social form as a demand for rights and freedoms – but without that once fundamental component of the demand for the right to own and control property without state interference.

We shall return in a moment to a more detailed account of these state interventions, but first we must see what happened next to ideas of economic liberalism. They never disappeared. Belief in unchallenged property rights, low levels of regulation and low taxes remained extremely attractive to very wealthy people, who were always available to fund economic liberalism's intellectual projects and keep its protagonists going during the lean years. Further, as the truth about the conditions of life and absence of freedom in the state-socialist countries of the east became widely known, there was a constant reminder for all of the dangers of state power. This was particularly strong in the USA, where past legacies of English rule and then rampant political corruption after independence had created general suspicion of the state. This produced a wing of political opinion that identified virtually all government action in economy and society with communism, and sought tough action to root out from public life all people who might be associated with such tendencies. In the 1950s this produced the highly intolerant campaigns on behalf of the US state, led by Senator Eugene McCarthy. The defence of economic liberalism had become highly illiberal. This contributed to the way in which the word liberal in the USA stood on its head, coming to signify support for the welfare state and other government interventions in the economy.

The fight-back on behalf of *economic* liberalism began earlier than this. Before the Second World War had ended, a group of German and Austrian liberals had pondered how to produce an economic order for Germany after the eventual disappearance of Adolf Hitler, an order that would recreate the entrepreneurial bourgeoisie that they saw as being crushed equally by communism, fascism and the interventionist policies of the democratic state. They did not share the belief that all state action was suspect, but saw a role for government in safeguarding the market economy in which they believed. They saw competition among many firms as central to the efficient functioning of the market, consumer choice, and the maintenance of a bourgeois class that would neither lose its place and be pushed down into an anti-capitalist proletariat, nor acquire the powers of 'big business', the giant corporations that were supporting Hitler. They were concerned that the outcome of the competitive process was usually the elimination of competition itself, as the winners took all and absorbed their rivals, resulting in the triumph of big business. These German liberals were attracted by antitrust law in the USA, which used law (and therefore the power of the state) to limit the share that individual corporations could acquire in a particular market, and thus to protect competition from its own consequences. The system they advocated was not one of unrestrained markets, but of *Ordoliberalismus* – an economic liberalism, whose competitive order would be guaranteed by law. To give the approach the name eventually acquired by its practical embodiment in much of the policy-making of the postwar western Federal Republic of Germany, it sought a 'social market'. In another of the head-standing twists of fate for political terms, this concept, originally part of economic liberalism's fight-back against the interventionist social state, had by the 1980s come to be used to denote the interventionist social state itself.

But these new economic liberals sought a role for the state, more specifically for law, solely in guaranteeing the effectiveness of market forces, not in pursuing other goals. Their ideas spread easily to the USA, where they became known as 'neoliberal', because liberalism as such had acquired such a totally different meaning there. There are now many varieties and nuances of neoliberalism, but if we stay with that fundamental preference for the market over the state as a means of resolving problems and achieving human ends, we shall have grasped the essence.

We must now consider how this return became possible at the level of practical politics rather than just as ideas. This requires some exploration of the other approaches to social and economic policy that grew up in the decades following the Second World War.

The Social Democratic Moment

Communism or state socialism, fascism and economic liberalism all denote very clear systems of policy direction. The approaches that emerged as their main rivals in the western world slightly before, during or just after the Second World War were more varied, as befits the role they played in finding social compromises among major antagonists, who in turn accepted the impossibility of either ultimate victory over each other or of knowing for certain what policies would be the most successful. It has recently become popular to associate the terms 'social market' and 'social democracy' with these alternatives. That the former is a case of head-standing has already been noted; but it is also partly true of the latter. 'Social democracy' was originally one of the names chosen by anti-capitalist working-class movements in the late nineteenth century. Others were 'socialist', 'communist', 'labour'. All were terms used, more or less interchangeably, by movements which had at some early point adopted policies for the suppression of capitalism and its replacement, at first by state ownership, but eventually, it was hoped, by an amorphous dream of popular ownership that would exclude even the state.

Following the Russian Revolution in 1917 the parties throughout the world that allied themselves to the new leadership of that country more or less all took the name 'communist'. The other terms did not acquire any differentiated connotations until the 1950s, when both the Swedish and German workers' parties, which happened to be called 'social democratic', abandoned the formal goal of superseding capitalism and proclaimed instead that their object was to work within an economy predominantly in private ownership. In 1959 German Social Democrats even adopted the slogan: '*So viel Markt wie möglich; so viel Staat wie nötig*'

('As much market as possible; as much state as necessary'). Other parties, such as the British Labour Party, had de facto reached that position, but were not willing to accept it openly until much later, the 1990s in the British case. From that time on 'social democratic' came to signify that kind of moderate centre-left politics. It still designated a particular type of political party, but by the 1990s it had, like its former antagonist 'social market' come to be used more generally to indicate a policy approach occupying some of the large compromise ground between a pure market and a primarily state-owned economy. During the third quarter of the twentieth century one could contain most of the political spectrum, at least of west European countries, within the terrain now so loosely called social democratic. However, outside the Nordic countries, Social Democratic parties as such only occasionally dominated governments anywhere in the world.

'Social democratic' has therefore now joined 'conservative' and 'liberal' as existing in an upper-case and lower-case form: Social Democratic, Conservative and Liberal indicate political parties or other formal organizations; social democratic, conservative and liberal indicate far broader sets of ideas, policy approaches and mind sets.

Seen in this sense, social democracy covers all strategies for combining government power *with* the market to try to produce an economy that maximizes efficiency in a manner consistent with the avoidance of major manmade shocks, with the pursuit of certain social goals that seem difficult to achieve through the market alone, and with limitation of the inequalities that result from market processes. Sometimes, though perhaps not as often as many assume, the goals of efficiency and reducing inequalities are in tension with each other. They are also, however, interdependent. Countries with extreme inequalities lack a large base of prosperous consumers who can sustain demand in the economy, as well as large numbers of people with sufficient economic security to develop the critical and innovative attitudes on which dynamism and ultimately efficiency belong. It is because of that interdependence that social democracy was able to define a wide range of social compromises; it is because of the underlying tension among them that the respective bounds of the market and of state adjustments to it became the principal bones of political contention throughout the twentieth century and on into the twenty-first.

One of the reasons why nineteenth- and early twentieth-century elites had taken a fearful and pessimistic view of democracy was that they could not see how mass prosperity could be achieved quickly enough to satisfy the demands of a literally hungry populace before the anger of that populace would have dismantled property rights. The more optimistic elites, such as the British, saw hope in a gradual, simultaneous expansion of both property-ownership and citizenship, the former being aided by the growing wages and stability of skilled manual workers, the increasing ranks of office workers and phenomena like the building society movement that slowly spread residential property-ownership.

But the problem was not only that workers were poor and lacked property. Their lives were also deeply insecure, as the growing market economy was subject to wide fluctuations. Late nineteenth-century social policy, starting in Germany and gradually spreading to France, the Austrian empire, Britain and elsewhere, tried to put a basic floor under this insecurity, providing insurance-based protection against loss of income through unemployment, sickness and old age. The ambitions, scope and therefore achievements of such policies were limited, but they were among the building blocks of what became social democracy.

These were the trends that eventually undermined faith in economic liberalism. First, however, it is necessary to take note of a more substantive answer to the poverty problem, and one more compatible with economic liberalism, which emerged in the early twentieth century from the mass production system of manufacture. This was associated initially with the Ford Motor Company in the USA. Technology and work organization could enhance the productivity of low-skilled workers, enabling goods to be produced more cheaply and workers' wages to rise, so that they could afford more goods. The mass consumer and mass producer arrived together. It is significant that the breakthrough occurred in the large country that came closest to a basic idea of democracy (albeit on a racial basis) during that period. Democracy as well as technology contributed to construction of the model. However, as the Wall Street crash of 1929, coming just a few years after the launch of the Fordist model, showed, the issue of macroeconomic insecurity (i.e., at the level of the whole economy) remained just as great. The problem of reconciling the instability of the market with consumer-voters' need for stability remained unresolved. In much of Europe tendencies towards both communism and fascism were strengthened. More moderately and consistently with democracy, beliefs in a need for governments to intervene to save markets from their apparent vulnerability to self-destruction were also reinforced.

By the end of the Second World War it was clear to elites throughout the then industrializing societies that the attempt to defend property from democracy through fascism had been a disaster. Capitalism and democracy would have to be interdependent, at least in those parts of the world where popular movements could not be easily crushed. The virtuous spiral of the Fordist model of mass production technology linked to rising wages and therefore to rising mass consumption and more demand for mass-produced goods was part of the answer. The more extensive approach to social policy of the kind then emerging in the Scandinavian and British welfare states addressed the problem of insecurity. Confident, secure, working-class consumers, far from being a threat to capitalism, could enable an expansion of markets and profits on an unprecedented scale. Capitalism and democracy became interdependent.

A further element played a major role in sustaining this emergent model: what became generally known as Keynesian demand management, after the British economist John Maynard Keynes, though the ideas developed more generally from groups of British and Swedish economists. They were mainly pursued in the Scandinavian countries, the UK,

Austria and, to a lesser extent, the USA, but were also taken up by international agencies like the World Bank, and for three decades constituted a kind of orthodoxy across the western capitalist world. In times of recession, when confidence was low, governments would go into debt in order to stimulate the economy with their own spending. In times of inflation, when demand was excessive, they would reduce their spending, pay off their debts and reduce aggregate demand. The model implied large state budgets, to ensure that changes within them would have an adequate effect at the level of the national economy. For the British and some other economies this possibility occurred only with the vast rise in military expenditure required by the Second World War. Previous wars had seen large rises in state spending, always followed by a major reduction afterwards. World War II was different, in that when it ended, military spending was replaced by expenditure on the new, growing welfare state.

The Keynesian model protected ordinary people from the rapid fluctuations of the market that had brought instability to their lives, smoothing the trade cycle and enabling them gradually to become confident mass consumers of the products of a therefore equally confident mass-production industry. Unemployment was reduced to very low levels. The welfare state not only provided instruments of demand management for governments, but also brought real services in areas of major importance to people outside the framework of the market. Keynesianism was not hostile to markets or to capitalism. Arm's-length demand management plus the welfare state protected the rest of the capitalist economy from major shocks to confidence, from more detailed government intervention in markets and from attacks from hostile political forces, while the lives of working people were protected from the vagaries of the market. It was a true social compromise.

A final component of the postwar demand management model was neo-corporatist industrial relations. This had not been anticipated in Keynes's own writings, and it featured hardly at all in US and only fitfully in British approaches; but it was fundamental to the Nordic, Dutch and Austrian cases. Under neo-corporatist industrial relations trade unions and employers' associations try to ensure that their agreements do not have inflationary implications, particularly for export prices. This can work only if these organizations have sufficient authority over all firms and workers to ensure that the terms of the deal are not significantly broken. The countries where this kind of collective bargaining became particularly important were all small economies, heavily dependent on foreign trade. Broadly similar arrangements developed in Germany, the only large country involved, as part of the priority on export- as opposed to domestic-led growth of that economy. Further, in Germany the union movement has been dominated by one large organization in the steel and engineering sectors and is therefore particularly sensitive to export prices.

These then were the principal ingredients of the socioeconomic order that came eventually to be called social democratic, without initial capital letters:

- Keynesian demand management in which government action, far from trying to destroy markets, sought to sustain them at levels avoiding self-destructive booms and slumps alike;
- strong welfare states that enabled people to receive some services in kind rather than through the market and some forms of income not dependent on market performance or property-ownership, bringing diversity to what would otherwise be purely market-determined life chances;
- in some cases, neo-corporatist industrial relations, trying to balance workers' freedom to organize with the need for labour markets to function efficiently.

What went wrong with it?

Neoliberalism's New Opportunity

Keynesianism possessed an Achilles heel: the inflationary tendencies of its politically determined ratchet. Countries that had Keynesian policies but no or weak neo-corporatism

– before all others the UK and the USA, but by the 1970s France and Italy too – were highly vulnerable to inflationary shocks. Different groups of workers would try to protect themselves from inflation by bidding up their wages. Unless their wage demands were coordinated by neo-corporatist unions which could perceive the likely outcome of such competition, each successful wage rise would lead only to further price rises. In a fully free market such behaviour would be punished by declining demand for the over-priced products and consequent unemployment. In principle, the Keynesian state, noting the likelihood of inflation, would reduce its own expenditure and/or raise taxes in order to squeeze the inflationary pressures. But that would mean imposing cuts in spending on public services and accepting some rise in unemployment (in order to avoid worse in the full-blown slump likely to follow an inflationary period). Governments would take some action of this kind, but usually 'too little, too late', as the political consequences of unemployment and cuts in public spending were unattractive.

This defect of demand management came to be seen as an intolerable fatal flaw following the waves of commodity price rises of the 1970s, particularly the oil price rises of 1973 and 1978. The inflation that hit the advanced countries of the West, though nothing like what had been experienced in Germany in the 1920s, or in various parts of Latin America and Africa more recently, was seen as intolerable. Policy-makers were persuaded by economic experts to abandon Keynesianism in favour of a tougher approach. Full employment was rejected as a direct object of policy rather than as a by-product of a sound economy; instead, governments and central banks focused on achieving stable prices and bearing down heavily on inflation. More generally, powerful sections of opinion considered that the entire social democratic experiment with running markets and government intervention alongside each other had failed. Governments could not be trusted to put the soundness of the economy ahead of short-term popularity by risking interventions that weakened the ability of the market to do its work of rewarding success, punishing failure and allowing consumers to make choices. As we have seen, this intellectual challenge, the neoliberal challenge, had long been ready.

Initially, the main rallying cry of neoliberals was for government macroeconomic policy to concern itself solely with the price level, by controlling the printing of money. The approach was therefore known as 'monetarism'. There was some debate over whether, in a world where credit cards were gaining in importance, the supply of actual money was so important in restricting demand, whether money supply indeed measured the degree of liquidity available to consumers. These debates have been largely forgotten today, as has the term 'monetarist'. It is necessary to recall them when we examine what actually happened to credit during the following 30 neoliberal years. As we shall see in Chapter 5, neoliberalism actually triumphed amid uncontrolled credit expansion, not tight discipline.

The speed with which Keynesianism and many other beliefs in government support for the economy were displaced in dominant economic thinking by monetarist and then other neoliberal ideas was extraordinary. In 1974 the Nobel Prize for Economics was awarded jointly to Friedrich von Hayek, one of the authors of the original German *Ordoliberalismus*, and Gunnar Myrdal, a founder of modern Swedish social democracy. In 1976 it was awarded to Milton Friedman, a major publicist of monetarism and a professor at the University of Chicago, the main centre in the world for the production of neoliberal ideas. He used the reputation of the prize to engage in a highly public campaign on behalf of monetarism. Over four decades, nine neoliberal Chicago professors were among the 64 winners of the prize. In 1973 agents of the US secret services assisted in a *coup d'état* in Chile, violently displacing the elected Marxist government of Salvador Allende. The army general who seized power, Auguste Pinochet, instituted a wave of execution and torture of opponents, and installed a group of Chilean economists who had been trained at Chicago, the so-called 'Chicago boys', to establish a neoliberal economic regime. Acting as they could with all opposition liquidated, they were able to establish what remains the most thoroughgoing experiment in neoliberal policies. Friedman paid Pinochet a well-publicized visit.

By the late 1970s the Organisation for Economic Co-operation and Development (OECD), which had usually recommended Keynesian demand management to its member states, began to advocate free markets. It went on to encourage the privatization of publicly owned industries and services, the imitation of private business methods in public services – the so-called New Public Management (NPM) – and attraction of private capital into the ownership of public infrastructure facilities – Public–Private Partnerships (PPP). During the same period the World Bank turned from supporting government projects in developing countries to backing mainly private ones.

In 1976 the Labour government in the UK, in the midst of a major inflationary crisis, formally renounced Keynesian policies and accepted the recommendations of the International Monetary Fund (IMF) to abandon full employment as a direct policy goal in exchange for an IMF loan. In 1979 a Conservative government was elected in the UK under the leadership of Margaret Thatcher that abandoned its party's postwar commitment to Keynesianism, a mixed-ownership economy and a fairly generous welfare state in favour of monetarism, privatization, low taxes for wealthier people and a reduced social state. The following year the election of Ronald Reagan as President of the USA ushered in a tougher version of the same policies. There followed a major deregulation of the economy, particularly the financial sector.

In yet another of the cases of political approaches being stood on their heads that we have seen in all varieties of economic politics, a paradoxical casualty of this process was the US approach to antitrust, which had inspired German and other European believers in the social market. Under Chicago deregulation economics, US law would come no longer to see competition as a *process* that would maintain in existence large numbers of firms, near-perfect markets and widespread consumer choice. Instead, competition was to be seen by both law courts and economic theorists in terms of its *outcome* as the destruction of small and medium-sized enterprises, the dominance of giant corporations and the replacement of the demotic idea of consumer choice by a paternalistic concern for 'consumer welfare'. These profound shifts in the stance of neoliberalism have gone largely unnoticed by a public debate which remains obsessed with a conflict between states and markets. They will form a major base of the arguments of this book, but first we must complete our rapid survey of the extent of the neoliberal transformation.

The principal tenet of neoliberalism is that optimal outcomes will be achieved if the demand and supply for goods and services are allowed to adjust to each other through the price mechanism, without interference by government or other forces – though subject to the pricing and marketing strategies of oligopolistic corporations. Therefore, to take the initial case at issue in the 1970s, government should not interfere to protect the level of employment if workers bid up the price of their labour so high that demand for their products falls. If that demand falls, then workers will become unemployed, and as a result those who remain in work will be unable to increase their wages, for the unemployed will be happy to rejoin the labour market at lower wages. In that way the market will find its equilibrium. The protection of employment levels had been the central preoccupation of postwar demand management policies. Neoliberals argued that trying directly to do this would in the long run be self-defeating, as it relied on an artificial support for demand levels that would become increasingly inflationary. If people came to expect that prices would rise, they would seek to anticipate those rises with pre-emptive wage increases. This would necessarily accelerate the rate of inflation, leading eventually to major crisis and loss of employment. If, instead, government refrained from intervening, prices and wages would eventually adjust at a level that would, in the longer run, sustain a higher level of employment.

It follows from this that the neoliberal critique of labour markets did not stop at the macro-level of demand management policies, but extended in general to attempts by governments or trade unions to seek to set standards for working hours, working conditions and occupational pensions, unless these emerged from market competition. Otherwise their costs would push up prices, reduce demand and thereby create more unemployment. Neoliberals therefore advocated a dismantling of protective labour law and elimination or reduction of the burden of social insurance costs on employers. This part of the neoliberal programme has encountered considerable resistance whenever it has been attempted in democracies, since many of the protection and social rights it attacks are popular. It was not until 1994 that the OECD (in its *Jobs Study* report) fully committed itself to the dismantling of employment rights. The European Union (EU) held to a model of balancing a competitive economy against strong social rights as a so-called 'European social model' until it took a fuller neoliberal turn in the first years of the new century. By that same point, however, the OECD had begun to appreciate some of the negative consequences of highly flexible labour markets, and began to shift its position to a more positive evaluation of some elements of labour security.

It follows from the above that neoliberals are unequivocally hostile to trade unions, which seek to interfere with the smooth operation of the labour market. From their perspective, the only consequences of union action are short-term inefficiency and long-term unemployment. However, in democratic societies they cannot advocate making them illegal, as this would involve using state power in a form inconsistent with fundamental liberalism; and in most societies it would arouse a high level of conflict. Neoliberal governments can, however, ensure that no hindrances are placed in the way of employers who wish to exclude unions among their workforces.

A further target of neoliberal policies was a whole range of government actions that protected certain industries or individual firms from market competition. In some cases (particularly in Austria, France, Italy and the UK) this had been achieved through state ownership of firms or whole industries. While these firms used markets to acquire their capital goods, raw materials, labour and customers, their finances were provided by government, so they were protected from the full implications of competition. For example, if they paid their workers more than market rates, government would subsidize their losses. Alternatively, governments would leave them *under*-capitalized, because government, as the sole ownership interest, was not interested in profit-maximization, leading to an inadequate provision of the goods and services in question. Most of the industries in state ownership in this way had arrived in public hands because their activities were difficult to subject to normal market competition; they were, or had been at the time of their initial establishment, 'natural monopolies' – for example, the supply of electricity, gas and water, broadcasting, railways.

Neoliberals advocated the sale of the assets of these firms and industries to private owners, and tried various means of introducing limited competition into the sectors concerned. In some cases (e.g., telecommunications) technological change made this possible; in others (e.g., railways) services were divided up into smaller parcels and sold to rival firms – in the limited number of cases where competition on particular routes was feasible. In others again, such as water, neoliberal governments were content to privatize to monopolies, with neither competition nor markets. In such instances they advocated the establishment of a certain kind of regulation.

Where governments did not own firms but offered various kinds of subsidy and support to privately owned ones, neoliberalism sought the abolition of such support in the interests of establishing level playing fields and fair competition. The motive for these subsidies had often been to advance a particular country's firms in world markets. This strand of policy therefore operated mainly at the level of international

trading agreements; here, even convinced neoliberal governments, such as that of the USA, would sometimes prefer
national advantages over the pursuit of free trade. The main
achievement of this strand of neoliberalism was the erection
of the World Trade Organization (WTO) in 1995 to guarantee implementation of agreements reached.

A final target of neoliberal policies has been the range of
activities that historically developed in many countries as
public services. The distinction between these and the provision of goods and services by publicly owned organizations
discussed above is unclear. For example, in Germany and
the Netherlands the provision of postal services is privatized
and fully marketized, while the provision of health services
is seen as the concern of government; in the USA it is the
other way round. In general, 'public services' have (as the
phrase implies) been limited to the production of services
and not of material goods; and many of the industries discussed above as formerly in public ownership had originally
been privately owned. But these distinctions are not absolute.
There is a tendency for 'public services' to include those
services that are either fundamental to life chances (health,
education) or that are consumed collectively rather than by
individuals (e.g., defence, public health). Here we need simply
note that these services, while always targeted for privatization by neoliberals, have proved tougher nuts to crack. Measures to introduce private ownership and/or market forces
into them did not develop strongly until the very end of the
twentieth century.

The neoliberal logic certainly applies to them. If services
like health, education and security are provided in the market
by profit-maximizing firms, users of these services might
(unless the private providers are monopolies, as often occurs)
be able to express their preferences by their willingness to
buy particular versions of them and not others, or perhaps
choose not to acquire them at all, whereas services provided
by government might (though by no means necessarily) offer
no choice or even be compulsorily consumed. Further, profit-
maximizing owners have an incentive to maximize the effi-

ciency and cost-effectiveness of delivery, which might not apply to the managers of public services. The neoliberal preference is therefore for complete privatization and marketization, with firms delivering a service to private customers. Public services have often been too popular to permit this, leading to a halfway house whereby government contracts out delivery of a public service to private firms, with government itself being the customer. Another compromise form has been the public–private partnership (PPP), whereby government continues to provide the service through its own employees, but the infrastructure – typically, equipment and buildings – is owned by a private firm, which then leases it to the public service, which pays an annual rent. In a further approach, which might be combined with PPP, government continues to provide the service through its own employees, but these are expected to behave as if they were delivering a service within a private profit-making firm. This has been the main meaning of new public management, with users relating to the service as customers in the market.

A wide array of policies thus constitutes the general approach designated by the term 'neoliberalism'. They are very rarely to be found in pure form. The main exception would be Chile, which was notably not a democracy when the experiment was launched. Singapore is also often considered to come close to the neoliberal ideal, but it too is not a democracy, and government there has a large moral presence within the society, even if welfare is privatized and labour laws very weak. Within democracies comprising populations with different values and interests coherent, monolithic approaches of all kinds usually have to compromise. For example, while governments in the Nordic countries have accepted large components of the neoliberal agenda, in particular privatization, they continue to have extensive welfare states and powerful trade unions. These two potentially opposed forces come to terms with each other, with considerable apparent success. These societies continue to have strong levels of economic performance and of economic innovation, while also scoring highly on 'happiness indexes'.

By the end of this book a generally negative judgement will have been made of the neoliberal era. It is therefore as well to end this initial discussion by considering certain features that many people of differing political values will consider to have been positive. For critics of the general approach, these ought to constitute babies in the neoliberal bath that should be cared for in attempts to throw away the dirty water.

First, neoliberalism has provided certain escapes from government domination and has extended choice to ordinary people who had been accustomed to taking what they were given. This has been particularly important, as we are living in a period when party and parliamentary politics in general have come to be seen negatively, as a game among seekers after political office rather than as a forum for representing popular concerns.

Second, neoliberal approaches have tackled the problems of centralism and remoteness that are endemic in much government action in large, complex societies. Against this it needs to be recognized that neoliberalism has not always associated itself with local sensitivities. It does so in terms of local government in the USA, where history and stereotypes pit a left-leaning central state against rightist local politicians. But in that country it has also been associated with the triumph of big business against smaller firms. In contrast, in the UK the authors of neoliberal policies, governments of all parties since 1979, have seen local government and other local forces as sources of non-market interference in their own marketization project. Neoliberals here have been centralizers. In this, they have been on strong if paradoxical historical ground. The original rise of the capitalist economy in Europe ran alongside the concentration of formerly feudal powers in the hands of centralizing monarchs. If polity and economy were to be separated – a primary rule of liberal and neoliberal ideologies alike – then political power had first to be collected together from where it was spread all over society and concentrated in one place, where, if the monarchy so desired, it could be used in a market-friendly way. The issue of central versus local cannot therefore be automatically read as the same as state versus market.

Finally, we must return to the flexibility of the neoliberal paradigm. Particularly in the Nordic countries, but to some extent also in the UK and generally in EU policy, it has shown a capacity to combine with other ideologies and political approaches. It is important that ruling ideas show a capacity to do this, not just because it is a better guarantee that the diversity of interests represented in plural societies achieves some recognition, but also because of the abiding uncertainty of all human projects. We never know that one particular set of ideas contains all the right answers; even if it does today, it might not be equipped to face unexpected challenges tomorrow. Monolithic doctrines that are certain that they have a monopoly of wisdom and which crush all opposition usually end by being confronted by challenges to which they have no responses in their repertoire. This was the case with Soviet communism. Neoliberal ideologues certainly show strong tendencies in that direction, but the practical realities of life in democracies force them to compromise. The links remaining between neoliberalism and the broader historical liberal tradition mean that it can respond to that challenge. This will be an important issue in its future likely transfigurations.

To take the argument further we need to explore some basic ideas about the nature of markets and their limitations. This means moving to a more abstract level of analysis and coming to grips with some terms with which many readers may be unfamiliar, but which are important to a full understanding of the issues at stake. This is the task of the following chapter.

2

The Market and Its Limitations

At the centre of the neoliberal project stands a portrayal of the qualities of the market, in particular a contrast between efficient, customer-sensitive firms and incompetent, arrogant public services. In this contrast 'the private sector' is usually assumed to be some unified, homogenous zone of efficiency. This is odd, as a central characteristic of the private sector is its diversity. It includes highly efficient global corporations, as well as small and medium-sized enterprises close to their customers and local communities. It also includes the financial institutions whose behaviour nearly brought chaos during 2008–9, before governments stepped in to save them from themselves. The private sector also includes firms using sweatshops and exploiting child labour in third world countries; various manufacturers of shoddy goods; down-market cafés and restaurants purveying unhealthy food in unhygienic conditions; local building firms that never complete their jobs on time; telecommunications firms so large and dominant in their markets that they pay little attention to customers' problems with their services; computer software and satellite television monopolists who fight every attempt to open their activities to competition; mineral-extracting corporations that pollute the atmosphere and water resources; firms that conceal criminal operations behind a cloak of legal commercial activity; pharmaceutical concerns which pass off minor improvements in medicines as major new advances. There is no such thing as '*the* private sector' about which generalizations concerning quality, efficiency and customer-responsiveness can be made.

Neoliberals have answers to such challenges: consumers are free to accept or refuse goods and services. If a firm producing goods of poor quality continues to thrive, it means that there are consumers who want poor goods; government interference that insists on minimum quality standards denies these consumers their choice. If firms using child labour are thriving, it is because consumers value the low prices of the goods the children produce; if consumers don't like the idea of child labour, they are free not to buy the goods. The argument can be used to rebut any criticism of anything that takes place in the market. There is therefore a fundamental asymmetry in comparisons between the private and public sectors. In the former there is by definition a place for anything that sells. The public sector, at least in democracies, exists in a world of political debate, where any poor quality is material for criticism, and where criteria of values and moral judgements are applied that cannot be answered with the retort: 'well, it sells'. It is then illogical if the solution to problems of quality in public service is seen – as it almost universally is – as being to move the service in question into the private sector. That does not guarantee either high quality or morality – only transfer to a location where a wider diversity of quality is regarded as acceptable, and where moral criteria are irrelevant.

The way in which whatever happens in the market becomes an ultimate justification of itself, the amorality of the market, is not necessarily a problem, as it is difficult and indeed undesirable to sustain life shot through with moral principles at every step. However, when, as happens when neoliberal ideas dominate, market principles are erected as the principal standard of judgement for virtually all institutions, amorality spreads right across social life. Every time it is authoritatively argued that the market should be used to resolve a

, that question is pushed beyond the reach of ethical
nt: it makes money and therefore adds to wealth;
... ubjection can there possibly be to it? This may well be
what we want to do in a specific case. But how do we put
ourselves in a position where we can make a decision whether
we want to accept this criterion or not? The more that neoliberal thinking permeates government and other institutions, the more we are prevented from making (or enabled
to avoid making) such decisions. We must reserve some
important areas of life where it is possible to make principled
assessments; and this must mean approaching the market
critically and selectively, and not as a talismanic solution to
most problems.

If the market becomes our only source of guidance for
action, there is a further problem. Does it mean that we can
seek only those things that we can find in actually existing
markets, even if these incorporate many distortions, and that
we should not campaign for things not found in the market
to be provided by other means? For example, if the mass
media are controlled by a small number of large corporations, making available only limited choice, should we have
no means of raising a political demand for more diversity?
If we can make choices only through the market, this would
seem to be the case. It is difficult to defend this situation in
any principled way, unless it is argued that government
intervention is always and systematically worse than the
behaviour of firms in the market, and that therefore any
defects in the market are to be preferred to attempts at rem-
edying them.

In the next chapter we shall encounter a powerful form
of neoliberalism that comes close to taking this position.
Although in principle the market is governed by consumer
sovereignty, consumers cannot decide what products will be
made available. Only firms can do this. The consumers' role
is a passive one, limited to signalling by their offers to purchase that a new product is useful to them. For example,
consumers did not generate a demand for iPads; a firm found
that it could make them, and set about generating a demand

by clever marketing and by ensuring that it was an attractive product. Consumers then greatly appreciate the things that they can do with their iPads; the invention is an excellent example of the market improving our quality of life in a way that never happened in state socialist economies, where no one had an incentive to make anything new for consumers. But the role of consumers in all this was passive.

This is acceptable, provided there are many other ways in which ordinary people who lack the capacity to become entrepreneurs can request or create things through means other than the market; but if the market takes over more and more areas of life, the scope for doing this becomes more limited. And since the firm is the only proactive participant in the market, the more that we live in a society that privileges the market, the more we live in a society that privileges the firm as the source of any human creation.

But some advocates of markets as the sole means of making choices make a different argument. They argue that, if markets were pure, we would not experience such problems, and that it is appropriate to seek government intervention where markets are not pure. However, such intervention should be limited to improving markets, not to making other forms of provision. If a goal cannot be achieved by making markets more pure, then it would have to be dropped as a goal. In the mass media example this would mean action to open up markets to large numbers of new private providers, but not such measures as the establishment of state-owned media.

Social Democrats have typically had a position that goes beyond this, arguing that there are some goals which cannot be achieved in the market, and that we should be able to look to the state to provide them through other means. We are back to the German Social Democratic Party slogan quoted in the previous chapter: 'As much market as possible; as much state as necessary'. Early twenty-first-century 'Third Way' Social Democrats would say the same, but they have learned from recent economic theory and from neoliberalism to see more possibilities in using state intervention to improve the operation of the market rather than to replace it. An

28   *The Market and Its Limitations*

important example of this position was a document of the British Treasury *Microeconomic Reform in Britain: Delivering Opportunities for All*, published in 2004 under the name of, among others, Gordon Brown, then Chancellor of the Exchequer and later Prime Minister.

This document is concerned with the problem of 'market failure', and it sees two approaches to such failures: those in which government acts to make the market more perfect; and those where the government makes its own direct provision, because the market cannot achieve it. As John Kay (2007) has shrewdly remarked in a critique of the document called 'The Failure of Market Failure', both types of failure are identified in terms of economic theory, which cannot see anything in society beyond bundles of individual preferences. But government is often called upon to resolve conflicts over desired goals, or with goals that concern the conditions of our collective life together rather than the aspirations of individuals. Also, economic theory views human action as motivated solely by material advantage. Therefore, for example, the answer of *Microeconomic Reform in Britain* to problems of poor performance by public service professions is to establish targets and impose better managerial control; it does not examine the scope for strengthening professional commitment and values.

There are no good reasons why we should not use markets to achieve our goals, or to seek to make markets more perfect so that they respond to consumers' demands. In order to use markets effectively we do, however, need to understand their characteristics and limitations, and to develop further the idea of market failure. This still leaves open as a practical rather than a principled question whether an identified failure can be better remedied by reinforcing the market in question or by seeking a different route altogether.

Market Characteristics and Failures

What conditions are needed for a pure market to exist? When we have examined these criteria we shall be in a position to identify various kinds of market failure, defined in terms of the conditions of the market and not just plucked out of thin air as grounds for opposing markets. Some critics of the market would argue that I am conceding too much. Why take the market as the starting point? Much of human life exists outside the market and has no reference to it: for example, altruistic behaviour. As Albert Hirschman argued in *The Passions and the Interests*, and Donald Green and Ian Shapiro in *Pathologies of Rational Choice Theory*, the assumption that human beings are 'naturally' driven by an aggressive and calculating conception of individual interest is very vulnerable to challenge. I accept the force of this critique, but a good deal of progress can be made in criticizing the dominance of neoliberal thinking even if one accepts the market as a starting point. This amounts to challenging neoliberals on their own territory, and reduces the range and depth of the dispute that there needs to be.

The first two stages of the argument are depicted in Table 2.1. The left-hand column lists the fundamental requirements for a pure market; the right-hand column lists the weaknesses or failures associated with each of these. In a pure market all goods and services are traded according to a set of prices denominated in a single currency (or set of tradable currencies), with multiple producers and purchasers. No one producer or consumer, or small group of such, is able to affect the prices by its own actions; all participants are price takers; no one is a price maker. In that way the preferences of very large numbers of consumers can be matched against the production schedules of large numbers of producers. The market characteristics set the conditions for such a market. When it is achieved, there will be an equilibrium: a situation in which, barring exogenous disturbance (i.e. one coming from outside the system), no single item could be changed in terms of its price or quantity supplied without some loss of efficiency.

First (condition I), it is essential that all desired objects (material and immaterial) be assigned prices within the market. If this condition is not met, objects that might

Table 2.1: Required market characteristics and associated failures

Conditions for pure markets	Associated failures
I All prices are comparable; everything is traded	1. Inability of market to deal with externalities 2. Problem of public and merit goods 3. Existence of 'goods without price' 4. Transaction costs of exchanges
II Market entry is without barriers, with multiple providers and purchasers	5. Major, virtually immovable, barriers to entry exist in many sectors 6. Inequalities of wealth and power accumulate as a result of persistent entry barriers
III Maintenance of a high volume of transactions	7. Failures of confidence inhibit potential buyers and sellers from entering the market
IV Market participants are perfectly informed	8. Major practical obstacles to fulfilment of this condition; inequalities in access to information
V Economy and polity are separated	9. Powerful interests, created by inequalities generated by 5 and 6, become insiders to political process

otherwise be desired will have a price of zero and no firm will have an incentive to produce them. If they are produced free of charge, their production will be inefficient, as there will be no way of knowing whether the resources needed to produce them could be more efficiently deployed elsewhere. For example, assume that a computer scientist prefers to grow her own fruit in her back garden rather than buy it in shops from professional fruit growers. Her garden is well below the size needed for efficient fruit production; a professional fruit grower with such a small plot of land would have to charge prices so high that she would be driven out of the market. Further, when she tends her fruit the computer scientist is using skilled labour time that could be deployed more productively making computer innovations than doing low-productivity horticultural work. If she were to price her labour and her other production costs and assign a market price to her fruit, she would realize that it is inefficient; she would buy her fruit in the shops, sell her garden to a professional fruit farm, and spend more time on her computer science. There would be an all-round efficiency gain to the economy and everyone in it.

It is also necessary that prices connect *all* goods and services that are for sale. Although we often use the plural word 'markets', there is really only one market; in that way we can establish our relative preferences across a vast range of goods. This is achieved by using a common unit of measurement, or money price, for all goods, either within a single currency or across a number of currencies that are themselves traded within free markets. For example, it might not seem to make much sense to ask how many oranges an airliner is worth, but if both are available for money prices, it is possible to calculate that equivalence very precisely.

A second fundamental criterion (II) for the operation of perfect markets is that there be large numbers of producers and consumers, who have easy access to and exit from the market. Only on this condition can we make the mathematical calculations needed to demonstrate that the prices that result from producers' costs and purchasers' preference are optimally efficient. In the market the price of a good rises if there is a decline in production, because consumers compete for the reduced supply by offering higher prices. If the market is perfect, this price rise acts as a signal to other producers that there are profits to be made here; they enter the market, and their increased production brings prices down again. If there is only one producer (a monopolist), it will be able to reduce quantity to force prices up (and increase profits) without fear that other producers will enter. The market is unable to reach equilibrium. There is not much difference if there is just a very small number of producers – known technically as an oligopoly – as they can easily send signals about their actions to each other and, provided they fear no new entrants to the market, can sew things up between them comfortably.

For markets to function without oligopoly and monopoly, it must therefore be easy for new producers to enter them as prices rise; what economists call the 'barriers to entry' must in that case be low. Barriers to exit must also be low: if a firm is producing inefficiently, it needs to leave the market, so that the resources of land, labour and capital it was using can be redistributed for more efficient uses. Or, if customers do not like the products on sale within a market, they need to be able to express their dissatisfaction by not making purchases, thereby requiring producers either to reduce their prices or to change the range of goods they are offering. The debate during the recent financial crisis over whether some banks were 'too big to fail' was a debate about exit barriers. If a firm is 'too big to fail' despite being inefficient, then high barriers are erected to prevent it from exiting, and markets are prevented from doing their pruning work.

The market needs a large amount of activity in it if prices are to be set through the interplay of supply and demand. This is partly achieved by the criterion just discussed, but also by the willingness of players who have entered the market to keep making transactions (III). For example, if no one wants to buy isolated farm houses, estate agents will say that 'there is no market' in them, which means that it is not possible to determine prices. (More normally, there is a thin trickle of sales, so strictly speaking there is some market, but too weak to enable agents to make confident estimates of the prices that can be expected.) This will in turn deter owners of such properties from putting them up for sale. Without buyers and sellers there is no market.

Markets depend for their efficiency on sellers and purchasers having high levels of information about prices and goods on offer across the full range of goods and services on offer (IV). In fact, economic theory assumes that information is 'perfect'; that is, that participants in the market possess all the knowledge they need in order to allocate their resources efficiently. We can see why this is important with a simple example. Assume I want to buy a new car, but do not bother to make enquiries about which model of car is most suited to my needs, or to find out the range of prices being charged for particular models. I just go to my nearest car dealer and buy the first car I see. I am likely to end up paying too much for a car that does not really suit my needs; I have not used the market, and my transaction has been an inefficient one. I could improve my efficiency by making a few enquiries; the more I make, the more efficient I become, until I reach the point where it would be more costly to acquire more information than to spend a little more on the car. We must assume that rational individuals do not want to make inefficient choices, and are therefore motivated to acquire all the information they need when acting in the market; we would suspect the rationality of someone who told us: 'I want to pay more than necessary for a car; and I do not want to find a car that is suited to my needs.'

The final criterion takes us from considering just the market to its wider context: to the need for the economy and polity to be separated (V). Both historically and in theory a major threat to the pure market comes from the state, which has the power to intervene in it, disrupting its delicate balance of demand, supply and price. This interference can happen in two directions.

First, governments might, in the pursuit of other policy goals, use their power to distort prices or the allocation of resources. They might try to divert resources to the private benefit of political and government leaders, their families and friends; or they might interfere in order to have more money spent on health or education and less on alcohol. We may evaluate these two examples of intervention rather differently, but from the neoliberal perspective they both constitute distortions of the efficiency of the market.

Second, individuals and firms in the business world might use the wealth they accumulate in their market activities to buy political influence. They can then use that influence to win contracts or other favours from governments. This again distorts the market. It is therefore essential for the functioning of pure markets that strong barriers are in place to prevent *both* the political world from intervening in the economy *and* business people from intervening in politics.

Having considered the conditions necessary for the market to exist, we must examine the failures typically associated with each, listed in the right-hand column of Table 2.1.

Market Failures

I Everything has its price

The attempt to allocate a price to all goods and services within a single market encounters four problems: those associated with externalities, public and merit goods, 'goods without price' and transaction costs. It is not true to say that these have been ignored by economists in their devotion to the market, as it is primarily economists who have identified and defined these problems. However, some of the terminology they use in doing so seems remote from the everyday meaning of words. It is therefore important to get some grasp of these terms.

1 *Externalities.* An externality is a good (or a bad) that is produced by an economic activity but which does not enter into the cost calculations of those responsible for the activity. It is a concept that will be used at several points in this book, and it is important to have an understanding of what it means. An example of a positive externality (production of a good that cannot be traded in the market) would be the amateur fruit grower whose activities were written off as inefficient above. She can argue that she gets pleasure from growing fruit that is quite separate from any calculations of costs involved. That pleasure is a positive externality of her

fruit-growing. For this reason she rejects the argument that she would be better off if she gave up her orchard and spent more time at her computer.

Some positive externalities provide advantages that can be used within the market. We can consider two different examples on very different scales, but embodying the same idea. First, a bee-keeper whose hives are located near abundant supplies of wild flowers will do better than one whose hives are located near pasture, even though he has not contributed to the cost of producing the flowers. Second, American firms have an advantage over others in many international markets because of the role of US military power, the ubiquity of the dollar and the global spread of American English. This latter kind of externality is called a 'network' externality. It refers to a situation in which a firm gains advantages in the market for a particular range of products because of its privileged or costless access to a network important to the distribution of those products. An obvious example would be a provider of telephones who has a privileged relationship with the provider of the telephone network. As we shall see, network externalities are a major source of limitations in the use of markets in high-tech economies; the term is therefore a highly useful one, however odd it sounds.

We are more familiar with negative externalities. Environmental damage is the most obvious and by far the most important case. Pollution imposes costs on many people, but these costs do not necessarily enter the cost considerations of the firm producing the pollution. In fact, the firm operates more efficiently because it does not have to take account of such costs. For example, effluent from a chemical factory into a river may kill fish in the river and deprive fishermen downstream of their livelihoods. The pollution is therefore a negative externality. The firm could control the pollution, but that would cost money. Since the firm does not benefit from the fishermen's sale of their fish, why should it bother?

It is not enough to identify a negative externality in order to justify a demand that it should be eliminated. For example, in the above example, if the costs of controlling the pollution should turn out to be higher than the value added to the economy by the fish, should the firm not be allowed to continue to pollute? Alternatively, if the fishermen are the main people who would gain from reduction of the pollution, should they not pay for the firm's pollution controls? These are interesting issues raised by externalities, which we shall need to address in later chapters. There is also the problem that it is not possible to predict the negative externalities that might arise from a highly innovative process; if it is really innovative, then not all its consequences can be known. Risks have to be taken if we are to create anything new, which includes risks over externalities.

2 *Public and merit goods.* These differ from each other, but they can be considered together. 'Public' goods are those that cannot, by their nature, be owned and therefore cannot be made subject to pricing. These goods are defined by two characteristics: they are 'non-divisible' and 'non-rival'. The former means that their consumption does not involve splitting them up into individual units that might be bought and sold. The latter means that the fact that one person is using the good does not in any way detract from someone else's ability to use it at the same time. Fresh air is the main example. It is out there as one big mass and cannot be sold to us in containers; and the fact you are breathing air has no effect on my breathing it too. The number of physical public goods is small, as many potentially public goods can be destroyed by crowding – this is even the case with fresh air. We find more examples with abstract qualities, like happiness. We cannot divide happiness up into little parcels so that we might trade in it; it is indivisible. And, in principle at least, the happiness of one individual does not depend on the unhappiness of another; it is non-rival. There can be no market in happiness, so it has no price; therefore the market gives us no incentive to try to provide it – though this does not prevent firms telling us in their advertisements that use of their products will make us happy.

'Merit' goods are halfway public goods. The term is an odd one, an invention of economic theory, but the ideas behind it are familiar enough. Merit goods have two components: a divisible, potentially rival one that therefore can be bought and sold and have a price; and another one that follows the rule of public goods. An important example is health. My health is enjoyed as a separate thing by me, so health is divisible, though not rival, and there can easily be markets in healthcare. But there are also indivisible gains that we all enjoy from a high level of overall public health, in particular low chances that we shall catch communicable diseases. If it is left to individuals to provide for their own health in the market, they will under-provide it; they are rationally motivated to provide for their private health, but not to ensure that they also contribute to the overall level of public health.

Education is another merit good. Education helps the individual who acquires it – including in rival situations, such as beating other applicants for a job – but there are also general gains from there being an educated population in, for example, the higher level of economic activities in which an educated society can engage. This explains why in all societies with advanced economies education up to certain levels is compulsory and not left to the choices of individuals or their parents. Education is also non-rival if we think of it as giving access to knowledge, cultural and scientific appreciation. This ambiguity is what makes the politics of education so difficult. Politicians have to offer it as a general good to a whole society, while what individuals and their parents often want is educational advantage for themselves and their children over others.

3 *'Goods without price'*. While economic theory is happy to embrace ideas of externality, and public and merit goods, it has far more difficulty with the general human tendency to insist that some things simply should not have a price put on them. Should people be permitted to sell their bodily organs if someone needing a transplant is willing to pay for

them? Should a young woman be permitted to claim unemployment benefit if she refuses to try to earn a living as a prostitute? Should mountain rescue activities devote costly resources to saving the life of a stranded climber without making an estimate of whether the individual's life is worth the cost? Economists can point to the opportunity costs involved in refusals to enter the market in all such cases – that is, what is lost by taking one path rather than another. For example, the resources used by the mountain rescue team have been taken away from some alternative application. However, they have no means of dealing with arguments that establish moral priorities over the market. Economics can tell us that we 'ought' to do certain things if we wish to maximize efficiency, and it has good reasons for encouraging us to do this, since inefficiency implies the wasteful use of resources. But the assertion of moral criteria that we believe trump the market does not regard the opportunities foregone as waste, but as the pursuit of concepts of the good that lie beyond the reach of economic argument.

4 *Transaction costs.* The final point in this section is a smaller one, and returns us safely to economic territory. Attaching a price to a good or service means that a mechanism needs to be in place to set and collect the charges; making market transactions itself has a cost. The costs of running a shop include those of pricing everything, establishing a means of extracting money from customers, recording this process, checking the honesty of the staff, getting the proceeds to the bank securely and employing accountants to verify the whole process. Obviously a shop cannot rid itself of these costs by not charging anything, but there are parts of the economy where the calculation whether charging is worthwhile is very salient. A major example is the issue of whether to charge road tolls, the apparatus necessary for collecting tolls being very costly. Of course, if charging is not to be used, there have to be other means of paying for the provision of the good or service in question, and for deciding how much of it is to be provided and to what quality.

Not so small are the transaction costs involved in acquiring adequate information in order to make a good choice at the market. This overlaps with the market condition that is itself concerned with information, and is therefore discussed under point 8 below.

II Entry and exit barriers

5 *The persistence of barriers.* The market's requirement for low entry and exit barriers is simply difficult to fulfil in many sectors of the market. Discussion here will concentrate on entry barriers, though as we have seen from the banking crisis example, exit barriers are just as important. In many markets there is simply no space for multiple producers: for example, there seems to be room in the world for only two manufacturers of large aircraft, Boeing and Airbus. One firm, Microsoft, is completely dominant in computer software systems. It seems technically impossible to have more than one firm managing water supplies from any one river basin. Whenever there are monopolies or very small numbers of producers, with serious technical or organizational barriers to market entry by further competitors, prices and the quality of goods cannot be set by the process assumed in the mathematical models of economic theory.

While technical change has eased these problems in some cases – for example, the multiplication of radio wave bands has made it possible to have true markets in many areas of wireless and telecommunication – in some other important instances modern high-tech economies have greater problems of making pure markets than classic industrial ones. This returns us to the arguments concerning network externalities discussed above. Wherever competitive advantages accrue to the owners of networks, entry barriers are erected against competitors. It is a characteristic of certain kinds of network that they are more useful the larger the number of people connected to them. This gives enormous advantages to a first mover, the first firm to develop a network in a particular field. Even if other firms develop superior products, they will have difficulty selling them, as the first firm has developed a network that must be larger and therefore more useful than that of the newcomer. The text-book case for this is the story of the rival video recording systems, Betamax and VHS. Two Japanese firms, Sony and JVC, developed systems for recording and playing video tapes, Sony in 1975, JVC two years later. Within a few years JVC's VHS system had driven Sony's Betamax from the market. While there has been considerable controversy over the reasons for this outcome, one element was JVC's ownership of several retail distribution networks for audio-visual equipment, these stores stocking VHS only. Entry barriers made it difficult for Sony to access the networks necessary for participating in the market. Today this has all become irrelevant, as video recordings have been displaced by DVDs; as economists argue, in an open-market, entrepreneurial economy, product innovations often solve these problems. At the same time, they continue to create new ones. The greatest single example of a network, the Internet, has provided many opportunities for first-mover advantage in establishing monopoly products like search engines that everyone uses, creating large barriers against potential competitors.

A major reason why these barriers are growing in importance concerns the implications for product standards of high rates of technical change. When a standard is needed for something that moves slowly, it can be set on the basis of long usage, or widespread discussion and agreement, and applied by national or international authorities. Such is the case, for example, with standard weights and measures, the design of electric plugs and sockets, or the alphabet. Such standards are public goods. Individual firms cannot own them and exclude others from designing products around them. But where a need for new standards develops rapidly and is subject to frequent change through technical development, there is no time for an outcome through widespread acceptance or formal public processes. If a large number of firms offer different standards in the market place, but the need for interchangeability is strong so that there cannot be continuing choice among many options, then one will be preferred for its superior qualities, and the market will provide the standard rather than public authority. However, in many cases the 'superior quality' is merely the power of one dominant firm to assert its practices as the industry standard, not through competition but through first-mover advantage and the establishment of network externalities. No one can make us change the alphabet that we use, but a dominant computer software firm is capable of preventing the alphabet that we type on our computers from triggering a set of electronic symbols that can be read by others, because it has changed the standards that govern those electronic symbols, which it owns and controls. Only giant corporations are in a position to impose standards of their own, and they can do so in order to prevent competitors from entering the market with products that consumers might well want to buy.

Patents can be used in a similar way to erect entry barriers. The issue is not an easy one, as without patent protection firms have no incentive to spend money on research and innovation. Public policy attempts to maintain the balance between the importance of market competition and the need to protect innovation, by providing patents for limited numbers of years. New issues have, however, been raised by the recognition by courts of intellectual property rights, not only in inventions but of the mere identification of existing natural materials. This has been given particular importance by the ability of biological scientists to analyse genetic codes. Firms in the industry for genetically modified organisms (GMO) have been permitted to acquire patents if they succeed in specifying the genes of naturally occurring crops, which they believe they might be able to use in the future to produce GMO crops. This can prevent farmers in third world countries from continuing their traditional practice of saving seed from one year's harvest for next year's sowing, as they find that the right to use the seed in question is now owned by a corporation. Also, researchers from outside the firm are impeded in working on the same naturally occurring plants.

6 *Inequalities consequent on restricted competition.* One of the consequences of a high level of competition should be fairly low levels of inequality, as high profits and incomes serve as a signal for potential competitors to enter a market, increasing supply and therefore reducing prices and revenue. This does not mean that a pure market society would be highly egalitarian; high rewards would go to successful innovators and the possessors of scarce skills. There would, however, be constant pressure on these inequalities from the competitive process. Where barriers to entry remain high, this does not happen. As a result, high levels of profit and earnings can remain unchallenged. In the first instance these inequalities concern earnings among different firms, but they gradually affect overall levels of inequality in society through differences in earnings and, more important, wealth. This is a secondary consequence of high entry barriers. It is notable that the shift during the past three decades towards an economy dominated by giant global corporations, with growing network externalities and corporate standards, has seen a rise in overall inequalities of wealth and income in advanced societies, reversing a longer-term trend in market economies towards reduced inequalities.

III *An adequate volume of transactions*

7 *Collapses of confidence.* The vitality of a market economy will not be very much hindered if occasional commodities, like isolated farmhouses, are not traded; but if there is a widespread collapse in confidence, such that buyers in general withdraw from markets, discouraging producers from producing for fear of having stock left on their hands, the market as a whole will fail. Such collapses in confidence can occur if consumers fear that they are facing a major decline in their income, or a major increase in the need for a certain kind of spending, that will have to be at the expense of others. Economic theory recognizes failures of this kind consequent on what it calls exogenous shocks: a natural disaster, a war or an economic crisis originating in a part of

the world outside the economy concerned. It has more difficulty accepting that purely economic shocks can happen within a market economy, as the pure model assumes that buyers and sellers have perfect information. It is therefore expected that they will take anticipatory action against looming difficulties, avoiding sudden shocks. There are two problems with this. First, our starting point is never a pure market economy; we might be able to reduce economic shocks if we could establish one, but first we have to get there through an economic environment that throws up many shocks. Second, as we shall see immediately below, it is very difficult to have perfect information.

An economy that is highly competitive, but in which information flows very imperfectly, and which is therefore vulnerable to shocks, will create unstable economic circumstances for people who have to earn their living. In the absence of any countervailing factors, they may become highly cautious and unwilling to spend money in order to save against an uncertain future. If they do this on a wide scale, markets may collapse. This is what happens in major economic recessions.

IV The need for perfect information

8 *Practical problems in obtaining information.* In practice, the requirement that market participants are perfectly informed is hard to meet. The central problem is that, in a market economy, most information itself has a price; acquiring information is in fact a major transaction cost, usually the most important of all, and thus relates back to the problem of transaction costs discussed above. It is a problem that seems to grow in importance the more complex an economy becomes – for example, through the technical sophistication of products or of financial instruments – and it is therefore likely that it has greater importance today than in earlier periods. The issue for consumers is whether it is worth their while paying to acquire the information that would enable them to make fully informed choices; but in

advance of having the information they can rarely decide whether it would be worthwhile or not. In practice, therefore, the acquisition of information depends not on whether it would turn out to be value for money, but whether we can afford it in an absolute sense. In other words, we are likely to acquire more information the wealthier we are; as a result, the wealthy are likely to make more efficient decisions and therefore to become even wealthier.

This further helps us to understand why the present period is seeing a reversal of the decline in inequalities that characterized the first few decades of democratic history. The problem is particularly severe in financial markets, where the wealthy can afford highly skilled professional advice to help them in their decisions, enabling their incomes to grow much faster than those of small investors. Similarly, organizations are in a better position to acquire information than are individuals. This means that producers are likely to be better informed than customers (unless the customers are other firms), employers better informed than employees, and large firms than small ones.

The assumption that participants in markets, even wealthy ones, have incentives to acquire adequate information can also be challenged. In the 1970s the US economist Eugene Fama used this assumption to demonstrate that stock prices are perfectly efficient. If it can be assumed that investors are rationally motivated to discover all relevant information about a firm when risking their funds with it, it can also be assumed that the prices of a firm's financial assets, which reflects the outcome of these investors' assessments, tells us all that we need to know about the firm's performance. This insight made possible development of the share maximization approach to corporate management: all that CEOs needed to do was to concentrate on maximizing their firms' share prices. This in turn made it easier to develop the derivatives and secondary markets that produced extraordinary growth in the speed of share transactions and in stock values from the 1990s onwards. The prices at which stocks and bonds were traded became the sole guide needed to know what the assets covered by these prices were worth. The growth of these markets therefore seemed to reduce the need for information, other than the self-referential information being produced by the markets about themselves. This came to represent a higher reality than the 'real' economy.

But this process in turn triggered the financial collapse of 2008–9. Far from providing incentives to acquire information that would guarantee their perfect functioning, the financial markets gave participants a dangerous incentive to do the opposite. They came to believe that they could depend on one slender line of information – asset prices – to tell them all they needed to know. But these prices had become heavily affected by a chain of guesses and gambles, and collapsed like a house of cards when these unravelled.

V *The separation of economy and polity*

9 *The inevitable entanglement of politics and economics.* For three principal reasons the segregation of economy and polity that the market model requires is rarely present. First, government is one of the likeliest sources of remedies for the market failures we are discussing. Second, the market itself needs law to function: at a very minimum the maintenance of a currency and guarantees against forgery, the provision of remedies for breach of contract, and protection of patents and copyright. Some of these things can be provided by the market itself. If one assumes that participants in a market want to remain in it, and if it is possible to exclude from a market those who do not abide by fundamental rules of using honest currency, honouring contracts and respecting innovators' rights over their innovations, then the threat of exclusion should be enough to ensure compliance. But that kind of monitoring by insiders mainly works where the number of participants in a market is fairly small, so that they know each other and can communicate information about bad behaviour quickly. Small-scale and traditional markets often have these conditions and make few demands

on law, but not the most efficient and extensive markets and certainly not global ones. One of the advantages of the market over other forms of coordinating action is that it enables us to trade with people who are totally anonymous to us, over large distances. Such markets cannot make use of interpersonal knowledge, but need mechanisms that enable us to deal with total strangers. It is interesting to see how the trading site, eBay, has managed to recreate something of a community economy at the highly anonymous level of the Internet, by strongly encouraging its users to rate the quality of the buyers and sellers with whom they interact. This is an example of how the market can solve its own problems without external intervention, but eBay users still see themselves as constituting a kind of pioneering community. It is difficult to see such devices leading to a general decline in the mundane need for contract law.

In fact, law intervenes even earlier. We cannot make contracts and claim a right to have them fulfilled unless we can claim a legal right to own property, as damages for breach of contract are assessed in terms of damage to property rights. Rewards earned in the performance of contracts can only be defended as earnings if there is a means of claiming them as a definable property right. This is something that many US citizens find difficult to understand, as their national foundation myth sees property as something won from the Wild West by pioneers' own efforts, and subsequently defended by their own force of arms. (The role of the US government in allocating land to the pioneers is forgotten.) The myth, propagated by countless movies, has been important in sustaining Americans both in their insistence on carrying firearms and in their belief that they do not need government to run a market economy. But the lie is given to the myth by the extensive and extremely lucrative activity of contract lawsuits in that country. Further, as William Roy showed in his book on the rise of US capitalism, *Socializing Capital*, capitalist markets developed only after the state socialized and underwrote some of the risks involved in launching major capital projects.

Finally, however, there are more negative entanglements between government and market. In a free economy it is very difficult to prevent economic wealth from being converted into political influence. The wealthy can use their resources to finance politicians and parties who agree with them, or to persuade those who disagree to change their minds. They can also run campaigns to influence public opinion, even owning and controlling newspapers and telecommunications channels to help them. Sadly, democracy and the market economy, far from inhibiting the political power of the rich, as each of them aspire in their different ways to do, both make the problem highly intractable. Mass democracy requires enormous resources to mobilize opinion; the opinions may be those of the many, but the resources to mobilize them belong mainly to the wealthy few. The market system may depend on the separation of economy and polity, but it can do nothing to prevent the rewards earned in the former from being deployed in the latter – partly in order to secure privileges in the economy in turn. Political power and economic wealth are mutually convertible currencies. This becomes a further means by which inequalities can be enhanced in market societies. Concentrations of wealth – the origins of which we have already seen in other market failures – bring a small number of individuals and corporations to the point where they can buy political influence; this influence can then be used to make them richer still; and this wealth can in turn be used to secure more influence, and so on.

Of all the market failures, therefore, those that tend to favour massive concentrations of wealth are the most worrying, as in the end they can be used to undermine the market itself and the reality of democracy. As we have seen at several points above, such concentrations are encouraged by several distinctive features of the contemporary economy.

The next logical step in our argument would seem to be to consider ways in which public policy has been used to tackle these various market failures. There is, however, an important intermediate step. We have been operating with the model of pure markets derived from neoclassical economic theory. This model is unrealistic in several respects, and some developments in theory have tried to address these, in particular concerning the role of the giant corporation which dominates its markets. The ability of government action to cope with market failure will be considered in the light of this adjustment.

3

The Corporate Takeover of the Market

> It is a fact that within liberal society itself one of the key divisions of political identity . . . is between these two sides: the side that fears private power more, and in order to fight it is ready to give more room to the power of government; and the side that fears the expansion of government power more, and is therefore more prepared to tolerate private power.
>
> (Amato 1997: 4)

While a close involvement in government and politics by all kinds of firm can cause problems for a true liberal economy, particular problems appear in the case of what we shall call here 'giant' firms. A 'giant' firm is one that is sufficiently dominant within its markets to be able to influence the terms of those markets by its own actions, using its organizational capacity to develop market-dominating strategies. A giant firm for our purposes is also one that is active across more than one national jurisdiction. Both definitional criteria are needed. There are today many examples of moderately sized firms that have branches in a number of countries but which are relatively small within their markets. Unless they have monopoly positions in specialized markets, these are subject to the full weight of the laws of supply and demand, and are not covered by the present discussion. The two attributes intensify our general concern in this book with the political problem presented by such firms, as capacity for market-dominating strategy can include having a political strategy, and transnational corporations (TNCs) can sometimes play off national governments against each other.

In the perfectly competitive economy understood by neo-classical theory the firm is nothing other than a nexus of contracts, a point where resources in a number of markets come together and are traded off against each other. The firm's behaviour can be discovered from the signals that the market gives to its decision-makers about the most rational path that it should follow, given its taken-for-granted goal of profit maximization. Firms that do not maximize rationally in this way will be out-performed by those that do and will disappear from the market. The human beings inside the firm are little other than calculating machines for working out the appropriate logic of maximization in any given situation. Economic theory and, indeed, practical commercial law in the Anglo-American tradition treat firms as though they were individuals, because these schools of thought do not have a concept of an organization with internal complexities. But actually existing capitalist economies do not conform to the pure neoclassical model. As we have seen, in many markets there are barriers to entry that prevent more than a small number of corporations being present in the global market, let alone individual national economies. Sometimes vast investment is required for research and development; or extensive distribution networks have to be in place before a firm can establish itself.

The fact that the firm, particularly the large one, is an organization and not just a nexus of contracts was first recognized in economic theory in the 1930s, in the theory of the firm developed by Robert Coase (1937). The central idea is most easily understood through the labour market. When a firm wants to make use of labour, it can do so by making a contract with some individuals that they will perform certain tasks in exchange for a set fee; if, when that task is completed, another one is needed, a new contract is made.

This is common practice for tasks that the firm needs only sporadically, such as formulation of a new advertising strategy. When firms operate in this way, they can be understood fully by pure market analysis. However, when they want continuous and repeated performance of a set of tasks for an indefinite future, or want to bind people who work for them into a shared culture, they are likely to find it inefficient to keep making new contracts and introducing new workers to the firm. They therefore usually make general contracts, known as employment contracts, under which the supplier of labour services is guaranteed payment for a prolonged period in exchange for placing him- or herself under the general authority of the employer, carrying out such tasks as the employer may require. This is the idea of a 'job' with an organization with which most of us are familiar. The firm here becomes more than a nexus of contracts and is an organization with a hierarchy through which orders are transmitted to employees rather than contracts made with subcontractors.

The main use that orthodox economics makes of the theory of the firm is in considering a trade-off that confronts companies. Use of the market enables frequent testing of prices and quality being offered in the external market, at the expense of possibly costly market searches and training to induct new employees and suppliers in the ways of the firm. Operation through hierarchy ensures continuity and reduced transaction costs at the expense of some inefficiency through neglect of market testing. Most large firms will reappraise the trade-offs in their use of markets and hierarchy from time to time in the operation of their businesses, adjusting the balance between them as seems more profitable. In several works Oliver Williamson (1975; 1985; Williamson and Masten 1995) has developed the original Coasian concepts, and in particular the idea of transaction costs, to explore a wide range of organizational issues affecting firms. As we saw in the previous chapter, a major transaction cost is information. Seen in simple neoclassical theory as something which rational actors necessarily possess, information is in reality difficult to acquire. One reason firms have for developing and deploying organizational resources is to be able to acquire information. Large firms that have developed the ability to act as organizations, choosing when to go straight to market and when to use organizational resources, have acquired a capacity for strategy. They have not liberated themselves fully from the market; they remain subject to it in order to buy and sell successfully. But they also have some ability to act proactively, to use their organizational structure to shape markets and to determine how they will respond to them. For example, instead of responding passively to market signals that there is a demand for a certain product, they will mount marketing and advertising campaigns to create demand. This gives them advantages against smaller, market-driven firms, and also changes their relationship with consumers, where these latter are individuals rather than other corporations. The symmetry between buyer and seller that is fundamental to economic theory in general and to the idea of the sovereign consumer in particular becomes considerably distorted when the seller shapes the preferences of the buyer.

These facts do not make giant corporations evil; which is fortunate, as it is difficult to imagine a prosperous life without them. But it does mean that they are not as fully subject to consumer sovereignty and market forces as neoliberal rhetoric claims. If we are increasingly told to welcome 'more market' in our lives, but 'more market' really means 'more giant firms', we need to know more about these and their political implications.

The Importance of Antitrust Law

The words quoted at the head of this chapter appear in a comparative study of US and European approaches to the problem of corporate power by Giuliano Amato, an Italian professor of law but also the past holder of several high political offices, including that of prime minister, in his country. In his book he deals with two of the central dilemmas in market economies. First, are the virtues of the market better expressed in the maintenance of competition, and therefore with the existence of large numbers of competing firms, as in pure economic theory, or in the outcome of competition, which may often mean the survival of a few giant corporations and diminished consumer choice? Second, if the former is preferred, and given that it usually needs anti-monopoly legislation to maintain large numbers of firms in markets that are prone to concentration, how much government intervention is acceptable in order to preserve competition? Posing these dilemmas immediately throws into confusion the hackneyed opposition of 'state versus market'. The confusion is caused by the insertion of that third entity, the giant firm, into the equation. Most political debate glibly assumes that the firm is part and parcel of the market. But what about the state and the market united against the giant firm? Or the giant firm and the state together against the market? Both are possible and do occur. In the above quotation, Amato is mainly thinking of the relation between firm and state, and eventually this will be our concern too. But first we must see how it is that firm and market become separated.

Classic US antitrust law, developed in the first part of the twentieth century, aimed at breaking up major accumulations of corporate power, so that there was a limit to how far any one firm or group of firms could go in dominating a particular set of markets. One of the strongest examples of this was US banking law, which for many decades prevented US banks from having branches outside their home state. The core theory of US politics, pluralism, was able to reinforce itself in this intellectual environment. It was essential for economic and political democracy alike that there should not be concentrations of power so strong that they faced no effective competition; ordinary people should always confront a choice that put them on more or less even terms with the firms or politicians who might otherwise dominate them. Further, there should also be scope for easy entry by newcomers into both product markets and the political arena. To the extent that economic power could be a major source of political power too, antitrust policy protected democratic pluralism as much as it did market competition.

It proved impossible to maintain all markets with low entry barriers and full competition, as the efficiency advantages of giant corporations, often formed through mergers between firms rather than by growth consequent on the popularity of a firm's products, became ever stronger. In their desperation to maintain the image of small-firm, small-town America, government antitrust lawyers were forced into ever tougher definitions of offences against competition, and government found itself intervening in highly detailed ways in firms' conduct. This was an affront to the interests of very powerful corporations, and also confirmed the suspicion in some areas of US political opinion that government intervention, even if aimed at protecting small firms and local entrepreneurship, constituted communism. Economic and legal theorists, principally at the University of Chicago, and corporate lawyers defending antitrust suits for large corporations, developed a new set of principles that abandoned earlier insistence on the need for actual competition and large numbers of competitors if the liberal capitalist model was to work. A new theory of the economy emerged, which tended to favour large, market-dominant firms.

Ironically, this approach, designed to keep government out of the economy, was thoroughly political throughout its development. The two academic lawyers, Robert Bork and Richard Posner, who played the main roles in reversing the bias of antitrust policy were appointed judges by President Ronald Reagan, and his neoliberal administration followed up these court appointments with various pieces of legislation favourable to the project.

We return to the first dilemma. Does economic competition denote a situation in which a large number of firms is present in the market, maintaining constant competitive pressure on each other and providing consumers with extensive choice? Or does it mean an economy in which competition has been able to work to its logical end of weaker firms being destroyed by stronger ones, with a small number of survivors and reduced choice for consumers? The classic answer of US antitrust law and of the German *Ordoliberal* theorists had been the former. It is this that was reversed by the Chicago school. One consequence was that the idea of consumers' freedom of choice had to be dethroned from the principal role it played in promulgating the US vision of the world. The new approach has never sought much public prominence for this particular aspect of its argument; the more general Chicago approach to a free economy without government intervention was popularized by Milton and Rose Friedman's television series and subsequent book *Free to Choose* (1980). But the serious intellectual arguments tell a different story.

The issue is not, argue Bork (1993[1978]) and Posner (2001), what consumers actually want to choose, but what gives them the biggest likelihood of having a choice. Logically, their scope for choice must be enlarged as wealth is increased in the economy as a whole. If there would be efficiency gains from a number of smaller firms being bought out by a larger one, then that would be the outcome that would maximize what they called consumer 'welfare', even if it led to reduced competition and left consumers with a reduced choice of goods. What should therefore be the concern of the law courts in deciding antitrust cases is what outcome would be most conducive to the maximization of consumer *welfare*, not *choice* as such.

While consumer choice is a democratic concept, leaving decisions to consumers themselves, consumer welfare is a technocratic one; judges and economists decide what is good for consumers. It is deeply paternalistic, the kind of idea that leads to the description of 'nanny state' when a government leans in that direction. If a group of consumers were to argue that they would prefer, say, to keep a group of local small shops rather than have these replaced by one supermarket, they would be told that they were irrational, as it cannot be in their interests to want a less efficient outcome. (In reality they are not asked, because in the market economy consumers do not have a voice as such, unless firms use them for their own private market research purposes; consumers indicate their preferences solely through price signals.) It is also a collectivist rather than an individual concept, despite the fact that the strong rhetorical stance of this entire strand of US economics thinking is individualist and anti-collectivist. Consumer welfare is to be understood in terms of a *general* gain in efficiency across the economic system. As we shall see below, the theory is not interested in how this gain is distributed among actual people. It is enough that there is net gain, somewhere in the collectivity.

This thinking favours the large corporation; at its core is the argument that mergers and amalgamations, leading to the emergence of giant corporations, will always lead to improved efficiency. The rationale for this view is that rational firms would launch takeover bids only if they were convinced that they could achieve efficiencies, and the prices offered for shares in the firm being taken over would reflect these expectations. Subsequent research has challenged these assumptions by showing that the improved profits made by takeovers might sometimes be associated with reduced efficiency. Particularly important are the network externalities and standard setting by large corporations discussed in the previous chapter. We saw there how a larger corporation can have superior means for distributing, publicizing or otherwise spreading its products, even if they are poorer products than those of smaller firms.

Giant firms also tend to possess considerably more information than their customers, except in those markets where the customers are other large enterprises. However, while this is very problematic to the idea of consumer choice, it is of no consequence to that of consumer welfare. Indeed, if having inadequate information makes customers more likely to purchase a product, there will be an increase in profits, therefore in overall wealth, and therefore in consumer welfare itself.

Against the advice of Chicago economists, consumer legislation frequently chases after these practices, as parliaments legislate for common standards of information, or the European Commission insists that firms in these so-called 'network' industries allow competitors to connect to their platforms. But the very fact of this chase demonstrates how firms will behave if left to themselves, and how they do behave as they discover new fields in which to use standards, not as a form of consumer protection, but as a means of profit maximization against the felt interests of consumers – but not their 'welfare', as the definitional trick has it.

Both classic US and European antitrust thinking had in mind a number of interests that have to be served by the structure of the economic order: shareholders, certainly, but also consumers as such, and the desirability of maintaining a class of small and medium-sized entrepreneurs. This need to serve a number of interests created dilemmas for competition law. Whose interests should be protected? Those of shareholders in seeking mergers sufficiently large to enable a firm to impose standards on a market, or those of smaller firms using networks or standards in order to enter the market, or consumers wanting to be able to maximize their choices? Anglo-American law, as developed under neoliberal influence, has simplified this dilemma considerably: shareholders alone constitute the interest that must be served by an enterprise. We shall encounter a number of problems with this argument below and in later chapters, but for the present we must concentrate on the aspect that is relevant to the Chicago amendment to antitrust theory and its approach to consumers.

The argument in favour of shareholder interests works well, all other things being equal, if perfect competition can be assumed. In a pure market, shareholders can maximize their interests only if consumers are being well served, otherwise these will defect to competitors. However, once there is a movement to the restricted competition characteristic of the modern economy, the situation changes. There are important asymmetries of information between large corporations and all others on the market. It is in the space opened by these asymmetries that there is scope for behaviour that maximizes shareholder interests but not those of consumers. It cannot therefore be assumed that consumer interests can be safely entrusted to the maximization of shareholder interests.

We can take this further if we are able to demonstrate the possibility of a decline in concern for customers by firms that are making high levels of distributed profits. We should assume that firms will do as much as they can to conceal any such actions, by maintaining front-line activities and cutting back on less obvious aspects of customer service – just as governments making cuts in public spending try to spare highly visible front-line staff in schools and hospitals. Reductions will be most evident where firms reduce their level of something called 'redundant capacity'. This is a concept that we derive from engineering, but it has many social uses. When engineers design a machine, they have to envisage stresses and strains to which it might be subject on exceptional occasions. Let us take the example of a bridge. If the engineers design a bridge so that it will take the strains of its expected everyday traffic only, there could be a disaster if ever an unusually heavy lorry tries to cross during already heavy traffic. They will therefore design for considerably larger stresses than normally experienced. However, this does not mean they can design the bridge so that no weight of traffic would ever be too heavy for it, for that would make it far too costly, drawing resources away from other projects with more urgent needs. A decision of calculated risk has to be made, and part of the skill of engineers lies in making these calculations. The extra capacity that the engineers design into the bridge, running from expected everyday traffic to the maximum possible load for which they decide they must design, is called redundant capacity. Most of the time, possibly for all its life, that extra load-bearing capacity of the bridge will not be needed; it will be redundant. Above that level is the risk that the engineers have calculated that they must take if the project is to be commercially viable. Exactly where to set the level remains a matter of judgement and cannot be delegated to a technical formula.

A vast real-life example of this issue occurred with the British Petroleum oil-rig disaster off the coast of the southern USA in 2010. All drilling for oil, but especially that from under the sea, entails considerable risks of accident and of potentially extensive pollution – major examples of what was discussed in the previous chapter as 'negative externalities'. Oil firms have to design into their equipment and drilling platforms expensive protection against a series of possible disasters that are unlikely to happen, but which if they do happen will cause major problems. They have to design for a high level of redundant capacity. This is obviously a highly expensive business, and the question has to be faced of just how unlikely a risk has to be before a firm can decide to ignore it and save some money. BP and its US subcontractors, including Halliburton, a major contractor of the US government in Iraq, made a series of such decisions; the disaster did happen; and the damage has been far greater than the cost of providing protection against it.

In the years preceding the disaster, BP and its subcontractors, in common with many other corporations, had reduced the role of engineers in their decision-making structures in favour of finance specialists. Engineers and financial experts take different approaches to risk. Did this change lead to a reduction in the degree of redundant capacity that BP and its US partners considered necessary? There was very considerable anger in the USA that such a disaster could occur on the US coastline, and the fact that BP is a 'foreign' firm loomed large in that anger. In general political discussion, US public opinion is usually scornful of the apparently higher sensitivity to risk shown by European publics as evidence of a lack of entrepreneurialism. It will be interesting to see if this attitude is revised as a result of this case.

An example of the use of the idea of redundant capacity outside the scope of engineering itself would be the funding of basic scientific research by governments. If government funds only that level of research that is necessary for easily perceived current needs, there will be no new discoveries, the potential value of which is not known at the time. Basic research, in contrast, generates knowledge that is 'redundant', as it cannot immediately be used; but one day it might become useful. Governments cannot be expected to fund all possible kinds of research on the grounds that one day it might be useful, as it would be too costly. They have to make a judgement somewhere between catering only for easily predictable needs and doing everything possible.

Redundant capacity is one of the areas in which firms can make decisions that will be immediately relevant to shareholders' interests, but only of clear relevance to customers' (and therefore long-term shareholders') interests in a longer run. A decision to reduce redundant capacity will immediately boost profits. In the longer run it might result in disastrous service failures, but if the firm fails to meet the share market's profit expectations there will be no long term, at least not for current management. Judgement is required, and the firm must choose between favouring shareholders or consumers; the more the firm concerned is protected from competition by near-monopoly status, the more it will lean towards the former.

The Chicago approach has three ripostes to these objections. These are arguments concerning the effectiveness of limited competition, distributive effects and government intervention.

First, it points out that there can be aggressive competition between a small number of giant firms. Once actual consumer choice and the market weakness of consumers is devalued in importance, all that matters for competition to exist is that a small number of producers are trying to take each other's market share. The Chicago school has reached the view that three firms will be enough to ensure this. If there are just two firms, and certainly if there is only one, the school would accept a case in favour of breaking up the firms concerned as in the normal antitrust solution. Critics argue that this ignores the scope for tacit collaboration among such a small number of firms. Assume, for example, that the banks in a particular country would find it more profitable for their shareholders to reduce the number of branches and reduce the training given to their counter staff, reducing overall the quality of service offered to small retail customers. In a strongly competitive market, with large numbers of banks, the first banks to try this would be likely to lose customers to more customer-friendly rivals, with consequent loss of profits; shareholders' interests are made equivalent to those of customers through the market. The banks cannot solve the problem by making an agreement to reduce the service offered, for such an agreement would break competition law, while with a large number of banks it would not be possible to maintain a purely informal 'nods and winks' agreement against opportunistic defection.

Now assume that the national banking system is dominated by four large banks. Their numbers are small enough to operate through informal, virtually undetectable signals to each other that they will all reduce services to customers and increase their profits. The capacity for strategy that a large player in a market possesses also extends to a small group of players being able to give subtle signals that cannot be detected by competition authorities. The Chicago writers are very dismissive of the possibilities for firms to give signals of this kind, which has led to them being criticized in turn for naivety in underestimating firms' capacities in this regard. Their argument is not based on naivety, however, but on the weight they place on a different factor altogether. What they actually say is that, while it is possible that firms engage in such practices, it is better to give them the benefit of doubt; otherwise one provides government with an excuse for intervening in the market, which the Chicago writers regard as the worst possible outcome.

Before considering this last fundamental point in detail, we must examine the remaining issue, distributive effects, as this also has implications for government intervention. The Chicago school sees consumer welfare as maximized when the overall level of wealth is raised in an economy, on the grounds that consumers' welfare cannot be increased by reducing the quantity of resources. They are explicitly uninterested in the distribution of this wealth, in who actually holds it. To take an extreme case, imagine a set of mergers that increases efficiency in an industry but which reduces competition to the point where prices to consumers rise, or services to customers deteriorate as suggested above in the example of declining redundant capacity. Provided the quantity of wealth produced for shareholders by the efficiency gains is greater than that lost to consumers through the increased prices, Chicago followers would argue that the price rise is consistent with an increase in consumers' welfare, as the economy overall is richer. If pressed on whether it matters if the actual wealth is held by shareholders or spread among consumers, they would probably say that much of it is bound to 'trickle down' to everyone else; but more importantly they would certainly argue that this is merely a distributive question and of no concern to economic theory. They might acknowledge that we may have reasons for caring about distribution, but would then say that this is a matter for political action, not for economics.

The Paradox of Government in Neoliberal Thinking

However, while Chicago economists suggest political action as the only remedy for distributive problems and, indeed, any other goals that cannot be achieved by the maximization of shareholder interests, they generally regard it as the worst possible eventuality, even worse than restrictive, anti-consumer behaviour.

To understand the depth of this antipathy we need to understand the traditional US hostility to most government action, apart from military, and its most recent intellectual manifestation in the political science school associated with the University of Virginia (see, for a key text, Buchanan and Tullock 1962). This has been the home of the public choice school of politico-economic theory. This presents nearly all state activity as the self-seeking and self-aggrandizement of political figures and officials. For this school, a proposal to develop a public service should not be seen as having anything to do with the substance of the service in question, but as politicians and officials expanding their scope for patronage. From this they drew similar conclusions to their friends at Chicago: keep as much as possible in the market, away from the public sector. Important issues are raised here, and we shall confront them in later chapters. For the moment we need only to register the dilemma in which the combined Chicago/Virginia approach leaves us in relation to issues like distribution, pollution and environmental damage. We are told that these are not matters for firms, as their duty is to maximize shareholders' profits; if we want action on them, we will have to turn to politics. But when we arrive at the door of politics we find Chicago/Virginia people waiting there to warn us never to turn to politics for anything, as governments are at best incompetent and at worst corruptly self-seeking. We are therefore left with no capacity to criticize whatever firms do, provided they do not conspire together in obvious collective groups, no matter what damage they do to any interests or values that do not serve shareholders' interests. While this is presented to us as a matter of individual choice in the market, we also know that the Chicago school of neoliberalism has redefined this so that it often means, de facto, the preferences of large corporations.

There might seem to be a further paradox in that, while the Chicago school is deeply suspicious of government, it makes major use of law. Its advocates would distinguish sharply between law and government. It is, in theory, possible to do this within the common law systems of the Anglophone countries, where the law is (partly) developed through changing judicial interpretations designed to facilitate agreements between parties, without recourse to government. The partial triumph of the Chicago approach within the US, and eventually European, courts was achieved through judges taking a different view of antitrust cases, without government action – apart from such small matters as President Reagan appointing Bork and Posner to the bench in the first place.

The Chicago school argues that, often, even recourse to the courts is unnecessary, and that parties to most disputes over property rights can resolve their differences by taking an economics approach. The willingness of one side to buy off the other will provide a sure indication of where the balance of material interests, and therefore overall efficiency, lies. It is notable that most of the examples on which this approach to competition law has cut its teeth have been taken from traditional manufacturing and even agriculture and not from characteristically late twentieth- and twenty-first-century sectors. The key text, an article in 1960 by Robert Coase entitled 'The Problem of Social Cost' (oddly, the same Robert Coase who gave us a highly modern theory of the firm in the 1930s), is based on the hypothetical case of a cattle rancher and a farmer. The former permits his cows to damage the farmer's crops. This was normally seen as a need for the law to protect the latter's crops from damage. Not so, argued Coase. If the farmer is to gain from the rancher restraining his cows, it is in his interests to pay the rancher to do so. If the amount he is willing to pay is enough to deter the rancher, then that is the efficient outcome. But if the rancher finds the amount offered less than he can gain from continuing to allow his cattle to roam free, then it is more efficient for the cows to continue to damage the crops. There is no need for an abstract debate over entitlements and rights: the amount that people are willing to pay to settle a case, rather than abstract ideas like justice, should determine legal outcomes, as this ensures efficient use of resources.

There is room for ethical debate here: does it matter if a legal system gives up all idea of justice? But we shall concentrate on a different problem. The Chicago approach calls for a limited number of identifiable individuals (persons or firms) who can be engaged in making a deal. It is far more difficult to make such solutions work where gains or harms from externalities accrue to very large numbers of individuals, as is typical of many contemporary environmental damage cases, especially where those affected cannot be defined as a specific class for the purpose of a class action and who have difficulty overcoming the problem of collective action.

Chicago writers are aware of issues that might occur through corporations combining together formally as anti-competitive cartels or lobbying politicians. Although the Chicago approach has done much to legitimate the economic power of big business against customers and smaller firms, it would join the already heterogeneous consensus of social democrats and neoclassical economists in opposing the translation of economic into political power – though Bork (1993) in particular insists that small firms conspire together to lobby politicians as much as large ones. Indeed, he departs from the usual position of the US of support for local levels of jurisdiction against more central ones, on the grounds that local legislatures are more vulnerable than central ones to lobbying pressure.

Against Bork one can argue that small firms, with the important exception of those that have local monopolies, are more likely than large ones to be in pure markets, with profit margins pressed down below the point where they can afford the costs of lobbying in the US political system. They are also vulnerable to the general problem known as the logic of collective action. Assume a mass of individuals (human beings or firms) who each have an interest in working for a goal, the achievement of which will benefit all concerned, irrespective of whether they joined in working for it. It is not in the interests of a rational actor to take part in action to achieve that goal, especially where that actor is a firm in a highly competitive market. To take part in an action while competitors do not is to incur costs that the competitors will not bear, even though they will benefit from successful action. If some 'mugs' do participate in the action, those who do not join them save on costs but get the benefits.

Giant firms, with their tacit agreements to limit competition and capacity to check what competitors are doing, are differently situated. They are not small players in a mass action; their contribution can make a difference, and they may stand a good chance of limiting benefits to themselves. Paradoxically, the danger of mixing economic and political power through lobbying politicians to take action favourable to a firm or sector is considerably greater in a 'Chicago' economy than one with perfect markets. But the school has its own answer to this. The more that government becomes involved in the economy, the greater the range of issues where corporate power can be politically deployed. Therefore, they argue, reduce the economic role of government, and the problem will be reduced. Once again we see Chicago economists recommending that we turn to political action to resolve problems of distribution and goals outside the scope of profit-making, only then to assert that government should not in fact become involved at all.

The firms that benefit from a permissive approach to oligopoly are not themselves required to abide by the strict principles of the neoliberal doctrines from which they benefit. There is absolutely no evidence that the corporate giants of the USA consider that they should not lobby government in case this amounts to an undesirable mixing of polity and economy. Amato, in the study quoted above, points out that US administrations became particularly susceptible to Chicago reasoning and its tolerance of oligopolies at precisely the moment in the 1970s when German and Japanese imports were beginning to hurt US manufacturing, and corporate lobbyists were arguing that greater corporate size would help confront this competition.

Robert Reich, a noted US economic commentator and former Secretary for Labor in the Clinton Administration, has described the US corporate lobbying system in his book *Supercapitalism* (2008). He attributes growing inequality, increased job insecurity and corporate corruption as negative features of modern American life that can be traced back to successful lobbying. One example involved the scandals in the US economy at the end of the 1990s affecting Enron, WorldCom and some other firms. These cases did not concern a murky hinterland of the capitalist economy, but its very heart. Enron, a Texan oil-producing corporation, had become the seventh largest firm in the USA, and donated millions of dollars to the election campaigns of US President George W. Bush. It owed $64 billion at the time of its collapse in

2001 – an all-time record that lasted only until the following year, when the WorldCom crash exceeded it. Both corporations had their accounts audited by Arthur Andersen, one of the five largest auditing firms in the world, until it too collapsed as a result of its involvement in the cases. (For an interesting analysis of the case, see Froud et al. 2004.)

Corporate lobbying provided the background to these scandals. In the name of the free market, lobbyists had persuaded Congress to pass legislation allowing a firm employed by a corporation to audit the accounts of that corporation and also to sell it other accountancy and consultancy services. This had previously been illegal because of the incentive it might give audit firms to keep quiet about irregularities they found in corporate accounts, so that they would not lose lucrative contracts. This is precisely what happened, and quite soon after the legislation was passed: Enron had major irregularities in its accounts; Arthur Andersen audited them, and its staff found the irregularities, but senior management hushed them up because of the important consultancy contracts they had with Enron. It is to the credit of US pluralism that the scandal could not be kept secret; the matter went to the courts and several senior executives found themselves in prison.

A more recent example is the extraordinary lobbying campaign unleashed by the US health industry against the Obama administration's healthcare reform policy. It was reported (by the UK's *Guardian* newspaper on 1 October 2009) that US health insurance firms, hospitals and pharmaceutical corporations deployed six lobbyists for each member of Congress and spent $380 million campaigning against the policy. 'Campaigning' primarily means contributing to the re-election funds of sitting congress-persons. Although the legislation was eventually passed, it was diluted in many important ways. One – which raises issues to which we shall return in the next chapter – was to replace the originally planned national health insurance fund of the kind familiar in most European countries with an obligation on citizens to buy private health insurance, government subsidizing the contributions of those on low incomes. This provides compulsory, partly subsidized customers for private corporations.

Similar sums are being spent by the financial services industry to emasculate the Obama administration's attempts to re-regulate that industry following the global crisis brought about by its unregulated behaviour.

In 2010 the International Monetary Fund (IMF) claimed that during the previous four-year electoral cycle, US firms spent $4.2 billion on political activities, particularly prominent among them being firms in the high-risk end of the financial sector (IMF 2010). A former chief economist of the IMF, Simon Johnson, has claimed (2009) that the financial sector has now captured control of US government in a manner normally associated with developing countries.

The USA is not uniquely vulnerable to corporate lobbying. In July 2010 the European Parliament decided between two approaches to food labelling, designed to give consumers information on the health risks associated with certain ingredients. One was a prominent colour-coded graphic of ingredients, the other a small-print black-and-white list. Despite their clear preference for coloured graphics to present their own logos and publicity information, 11 leading food and drinks manufacturers lobbied heavily in favour of the small-print black-and-white lists. A representative of a consumers' organization, which was lobbying for colour-coding, told the *Independent* newspaper (7 July 2010) that corporate lobbyists out-numbered those of consumer associations by a hundred to one. The Parliament voted as the corporate lobbyists wanted.

Amato set out as the central dilemma of antitrust policy the choice between private and public power: do we risk enhancing the state's reach in order to tame private economic power, or do we tolerate the latter in order to avoid giving government more power? The Chicago approach seems to belong squarely with the latter; but in fact it does something quite different. By assisting in the growth of truly giant corporations, it connives at a mighty combination of private economic power and state power. The latter is not used in a totalitarian way, as with the fascist or communist state, but it is used further to assist and protect the interests of those corporations.

Much of the original extremism of Chicago antitrust doctrine has failed to stand the test of time (Cucinotta et al. 2002). In particular, its neglect of network externalities in fast-moving, high-tech economies, and its acceptance of the ways in which small groups of dominant firms can act anti-competitively without leaving any paper or email trail of complicity, have led to considerable revision in US law, and limited the extent to which European law has imitated earlier US developments. In 2002, Richard Schmalensee, an academic who had helped Microsoft Corporation fight its legal battles against US antitrust authorities, was complaining, just as Bork had 20 years before, that antitrust law prevented leading firms from pressing home their advantage, forcing them to allow competitors to survive with a resulting overall loss of efficiency. He attributed Microsoft's legal problems to the fact that it had not devoted enough attention to political lobbying – a situation which it has subsequently remedied.

It is a testimony to the strength of public institutions and a sense of public interest on both sides of the Atlantic that antitrust suits continue to be brought to the courts, and that corporations are required to relinquish a monopoly position or provide access to their platforms for smaller competitors. However, three major points remain. First, the paternalistic test of consumer welfare rather than actual consumer choice, and the essentially collectivist doctrine that, provided wealth has been created somewhere in the system, it does not matter who enjoys it, have remained central to how mergers and acquisitions are viewed in competition law. These concepts have become part of the heritage of neoliberalism, however true its rhetoric remains to the ideal of freedom of choice.

Second, whatever the defects of Chicago theory as a set of economic principles when compared with the theory of pure markets, it came into being partly as an attempt to counter the sheer lack of reality of the previous orthodoxy. By the 1970s US antitrust law, in its attempt to prevent market domination by giant enterprises, had started imposing impossible and impractical restrictions on mergers and acquisitions. Whether one sees this attempt to safeguard small firms and consumer choice as nostalgia for an increasingly unrealistic image of small-town America or (as Bork believed) as an attempt to impose a socialist state, it was certainly Quixotic. The same applies to the similar aspirations of the *Ordoliberalen*. The positive achievement here of the Chicago approach to antitrust was to make the courts, as well as legal and economic analysts, think seriously about the opportunity costs of trying to preserve the neoclassical ideal of an economy dominated by masses of small and medium-sized enterprises. Trying to maintain this ideal would be costly in terms of both economic efficiency losses and increased government intervention. But they could have made these points solely within the framework of that well-trusted economics concept: opportunity cost. Redefining the matter as the contorted notion of 'consumer welfare' was a piece of populist rhetoric which betrays the political rather than purely economic and jurisprudential motivation of the authors of that concept.

Finally, the Chicago innovations did nothing to resolve the central issue: economic and political power translate into each other. This is why it is so difficult in practice to maintain the separateness alongside interdependence required by liberal capitalism. An economy dominated by giant firms makes this worse, as it generates very high concentrations of wealth. Not only can firms convert this wealth into political influence, but they can use the capacity for strategy given to them by their size and organizational hierarchies to pursue political purposes and to become political actors. Seeing the firm as an organization and not just as a nexus of contracts enables us to perceive the implications of this for political theory.

4

Private Firms and Public Business

The previous chapter considered a distinction between the market and large enterprises, and a tendency in neoliberal thought to give the latter attributes of the former that they do not really share. We encounter this distinction again when considering the very important processes that have taken place in recent years as governments, under the influence of neoliberal ideas, have sought to move their own activities closer to those of the private sector or even to move them fully into that sector. The process is always seen as being about adapting government to the market. Often it has instead adapted it to the corporation. This has in turn further helped to develop the politicized giant firm – which is in its turn the opposite of what liberal political economy intended.

Much conventional debate over the relative virtues of the market and the state relates to the market failures discussed in Chapter 2, and the approaches with which governments have historically sought to remedy them. These approaches then became themselves the objects of neoliberal criticism from the 1970s onwards as the sources of 'government failure'. We are now ready to examine these, disabused by the discussion in Chapter 3 from believing that it is a simple matter of state versus market.

Table 4.1 recapitulates in its first column the market failures discussed in Chapter 2. The second column lists the standard twentieth-century responses of democratic states to these failures. The final column presents the failures identified in these responses themselves by the neoliberal critique, which led in turn to that approach's agenda of new public management, marketization and privatization.

First, the state sought to deal with negative externalities by imposing regulations (such as pollution control laws) which force firms and others to deal with the externalities under pain of fines and other sanctions. Neoliberals point to the costs that regulations impose on economic activity; they make the objection we have already discussed, that costs to the economic activity causing the externality also have to be put into the scale as losses to welfare. They also note the tendency of regulation to discourage innovation, as new products and processes need to be inspected and evaluated. They may also join left-wing critics of regulation and use an argument that tends in the opposite direction: official regulation is slow and formalistic, always running behind innovation in the market and therefore unable to deal with rapidly emerging externalities. It is also vulnerable to 'regulatory capture' by the firms being regulated; often the only expertise that exists about a field of activity is held within the firms concerned, so government is dependent on them for advice about how to exercise its regulation, which tends to weaken it – another example of the difficulty of disentangling economic and political power.

Second, the state dealt with problems of public and merit goods, as well as some 'goods without price' and the lesser problem of transaction costs, by providing these goods directly through its own services, paying for them through taxation revenues rather than through prices. In this way, their provision (though not their production) is removed from the market. This explains the existence of public health and education services, certain cultural facilities, and roads without tolls. Until the current vogue for privatization, states used to deal with severe problems of entry barriers in a

Table 4.1: Market failures, government solutions, and their failures

Market failures	Standard government responses	Government failures identified by neoliberal critique
1. Inability of market to deal with externalities	Regulation to enforce recognition of externalities (e.g. pollution control standards)	Regulation imposes excessive burdens on market; or is formalistic and slow to adapt to new problems; also regulatory capture
2. Problem of public and merit goods 3. Existence of 'goods without price' 4. Transaction costs of exchanges	Direct provision of goods by government, financed by taxation instead of prices to users (e.g. education and health services)	Unwanted services, unresponsive to customers; dominance of producer interests; high taxation; inadequate cost effectiveness
5. Major, virtually immovable, barriers to entry in many sectors	Direct state provision of goods and services where true market competition cannot be secured (e.g. public utilities)	
6. Inequalities of wealth and power accumulate as a result of persistent entry barriers	Redistributive taxation; free or subsidized provision of goods and services where inequalities are considered unacceptable (e.g. education, health, social services, transport)	As above; also, public service provision subject to lobbying from interests privileged by existing inequalities
7. Major practical obstacles to perfect information; inequalities in access to information	Decisions about service provision taken by well informed central policy elite	As above; also, excessive centralization and remoteness
8. Powerful interests, created by inequalities generated by 5 and 6, become insiders to political process	Public service codes of conduct stress separation of business and politico-administrative elites	Politico-administrative elites become out of touch with business approaches

similar way. As already noted, this was especially the case
with what were known as 'natural monopolies', where
the physical or technical requirements of providing a good
or service made it virtually impossible for there to be
competition.

For neoliberals these state actions present two different
defects. First, because provision is decided by politicians and
government officials, it is likely to follow the preferences of
their producers rather than of users, and they will be slow
to respond to users' dissatisfaction. Care services will have
opening hours that suit the needs of staff rather than of
users; schools will teach what teachers enjoy teaching rather
than what parents want their children to learn. Alternatively,
however, there is likely to be over-provision; because they
are producer-led and funded by compulsory taxation rather
than prices that people choose to pay, public services will
provide things that keep staff employed rather than meet
felt needs. They are also likely to be inefficient, lacking any
incentives to cost-effectiveness; and there will be little pressure to take the trouble to dismiss poor-quality staff. Further,
by requiring citizens to finance these goods and services
through their taxes, they necessarily change their patterns
of consumption from those that they would have chosen if
left to themselves, which by definition reduces their welfare.
If reducing my taxes by cutting back on a publicly funded
health service leads me to spend more on tobacco and less
on health, my freedom of choice and therefore my welfare
have been improved.

Third, states have to some extent tried to reduce inequalities resulting from market failures by a double move. First,
they have used the techniques already discussed of providing
certain essential goods and services free or heavily subsidized
at the point of use, reducing the need for prices and their
dependence on ability to pay. Second, they have levied taxation in a way that requires wealthier people to pay more.
Neoliberals here raise their usual objections to direct state
provision, but may add a further argument with a very different twist. Since governments are subject to lobbying, and

since the better off are better equipped to lobby than the poor, the distribution of direct state provision is likely to be as skewed towards the wealthy as provision in the market. They point to the way in which state schools in wealthy areas are likely to be better than those in poor areas, or in which the heavily subsidized service of higher education is mainly taken up by the children of the wealthy. In an argument tending in a different direction, they also raise the traditional objection to progressive taxation that it punishes those who show enterprise and create wealth.

Fourth, the classic public service response to market failures of information has been to transfer responsibility for handling information about vital areas to an informed policy and professional elite, which then takes responsibility for providing services and monitoring their quality. It then becomes unnecessary for people to worry what education to provide for their children, or what kind of healthcare to seek, or which fire service would be most likely to deal effectively with a house fire. In providing these services, government will also take advantage of its position of power to use the best possible information, in a way that is beyond the reach of the ordinary citizen. Against these points, and in addition to their general objections to state provision, neoliberals complain of centralization, remoteness and likely arrogance of a policy elite that assumes it knows best what people want.

Finally, the state has difficulty in dealing with problems that result from the mingling of polity and economy, as its own decisions to intervene to offset market failures breach that divide. What it has done instead is to erect codes of conduct that regulate relations between politicians and state officials, on the one hand, and private business people, on the other. Gift exchanges are either prohibited or closely monitored; forms of legitimate discussion are carefully prescribed; there are limitations on the ability of public officials to move to subsequent employment in the private sector, especially if they have been involved in the politics of the sector concerned.

Rules of this kind were the classic hallmarks of nine-teenth-century liberalism, reinforced by twentieth-century social democracy in its suspicion of mutual entanglements of business and politics. The desire of liberals to protect the market from politicians, and the desire of social democrats to protect the polity from businessmen, produced an unusual alliance. Late twentieth- and twenty-first-century neoliberal-ism departs radically from this consensus, as it criticizes the division between business and politics for having produced a political and public administrative class that has become remote from private business and out of touch with its mar-ket-driven incentives, and therefore unlikely to innovate or achieve efficiencies.

There is no space here thoroughly to examine each of these forms of government action and the validity of the neoliberal critique. Our study is focused on neoliberalism's own practices. We must therefore shift attention to the ways in which neoliberalism derived a set of responses to the public service weaknesses it identified, and to problems that have emerged with these responses. The government failures identified in Table 4.1 can be reduced to three main themes: unresponsiveness to users; provision of excessive or unwanted services; and a failure of the public sector to benefit from improvements in efficiency and service delivery being achieved by private firms. Table 4.2 aligns these with the proposed solutions that have constituted the neoliberal reform agenda – and then with the problems that have been found to accompany that agenda, as the dialectic continues.

'Unresponsiveness to users of public services' covers the neoliberal claim that public services are dominated by pro-ducer interests, as government policy-making is carried out by the officials and professionals who deliver the services; these provide what they like providing, which is not neces-sarily what consumers want. This is also a remote, central-ized process – particularly in countries like France or the UK, where local government is weak and most power lies with the central ministries. Also, public provision is usually

Table 4.2: Marketization strategies in response to public service failures, and newly emerging problems

Public service failure	Marketization response	Problems of marketization
A. Unresponsive to consumers; dominated by producer interests; centralized and remote	(i) Privatization, with regulation where competition remains imperfect	Scope for extensive marketization often limited by technical features; regulation remains a large public activity
	(ii) Market-making within public service, with direct consumer choice guided by performance data	Market failure; inadequate information, resolved by top-down control of performance data
	(iii) Private providers and sub-contractors compete with public ones, but within publicly funded system	Limited use of price mechanism; central authorities still control much pricing; small numbers of contractors; loss of responsibility through contract chain; long contracts inhibit use of markets; development of 'insider' firms
B. Unwanted services; inadequate cost effectiveness; high taxes	(iv) Internal markets	Limited use of price mechanism
C. Public service out of touch with business	(v) Adoption of business criteria in government practice	Limits to and inappropriateness of pure markets in public service
	(vi) Encouragement of intensive interaction with, and learning from, private sector	Development of insider firms, return to market failure of inadequate barriers between polity and econom

monopoly provision, imparting particular power to producers. The neoliberal critique considered that virtually all economic activity would be more effectively conducted within profit-maximizing firms with clear incentives to satisfy their customers, rather than provide quiet lives and aggrandizement for public sector producers – as had been argued by the Virginia public choice school discussed in the previous chapter.

This discussion assumes that the public wants the services in question, but seeks more choice and better quality. Another argument for marketization is almost the reverse of this: 'Unwanted services'. As we saw above, it has been argued that, because they are funded by taxation and decided by producer interests, public services are provided in 'excess'. A more consumer-oriented system might therefore be associated not so much with better public services, as with poorer quality ones. Several of the strategies that seem to be aimed at improving the quality of public services can also be easily aimed at this opposite goal.

For example, a private subcontractor might win a contract to provide a service by offering a low price, alongside the argument that the public will accept a reduced standard; and the public commissioning authority might be persuaded of the logic of this. Governments might, experimenting across a wide range of services, be able to discover where a lower standard is publicly acceptable, and where it leads to outcry. If the latter, the approach can be quickly abandoned. The approach may well identify certain aspects of public service provision which have become wasteful because no one really wants them. There is, however, likely to be another side to the issue. It may be quite acceptable for, say, a budget airline to reduce the space between rows, and consequent legroom, on short-haul holiday flights in order to get fares down. Can the same logic be extended to, say, the amount of space that people in an elderly care home have to move around in? Such an approach may well pass the market test; there may be little complaint from a group of octogenarians. Or at least, complaint is likely to come only from those in affluent areas with articulate relatives – in which the market-sensitive answer would be to allow more space to people in those homes than to those in poorer areas.

Arguments that services are being provided in excess are politically difficult to make, but there may be public concerns that there are inadequate pressures on public services to provide value for money, and people would still prefer to pay lower taxes. The most obvious way to square the circle of a demand for services alongside reluctance to pay for them is to improve efficiency. Governments have recently tended to believe that the best ideas for doing this are likely to be found in the private sector, which is more immediately exposed to competitive pressure on costs.

To these problems, neoliberal reform strategy offered a number of responses. Some of these, as can be seen from Table 4.2, deal with the use of internal markets and new public management within public services. These, the gains they have brought and the deficiencies they have shown, are not our main focus here, which is on the relationship between government and private firms. They will therefore be discussed only to the extent that they overlap with this narrower concern. We shall consider public service failures A and B (Table 4.2) together, as they raise similar issues. Then we shall tackle failure C.

Privatization With or Without Marketization

In previous chapters we have considered the need to distinguish between the market and control by large enterprises. We also encounter this distinction when considering the two concepts of privatization and marketization. Marketization implies offering a good or service for sale, placing it in the market under all the conditions discussed above. By itself, this does not necessarily imply private ownership of the means of production; it has long been possible for services to remain in public ownership, and even to remain delivered by public agencies, but for consumers to obtain them through purchase. The quality and quantity of their provision can then be governed by consideration of the prices that consumers are prepared to pay. Alternatively, marketization can be a process carried on within an organization, whether in the public or private sector; the markets that are imposed in such cases are known as 'internal' markets. Organizations of all kinds have a choice as to how they allocate resources among their different departments. There may be a system of decisions by the organization's leadership, based on certain principles and desired outcomes, often preceded by a process of bargaining with the departments; or the leadership may permit market forces to determine how these resources flow. Often there is a combination of the two, with market forces operating only after the leadership has fixed certain parameters, such as prices.

Marketization must therefore be distinguished from privatization, which refers to selling or otherwise handing to private owners the assets of a formerly public service. This, in turn, might or might not imply marketization; a public service can be sold to a private monopoly, with ultimate consumers having little or no ability to affect the provision through their market behaviour. An important factor encouraging privatization has been that it would enable governments to attract private finance into the funding of major capital projects, instead of relying on taxation or public debt.

True markets have rarely accompanied these privatizations, problems of oligopoly and limited opportunities for competition usually having been important reasons why these activities had ended up in the public domain in the first place. An example of unsatisfactory privatization to a monopoly took place in the UK in the solution adopted for railway track provision and maintenance, where privatization was considered to create problems of rail safety. The track was therefore placed into an unusual form of ownership, designed to avoid giving the appearance of renationalization, while also avoiding the market failures of a monopoly. An organization called Network Rail was created, which calls itself a private company acting on a commercial basis. But it was established by government, has no shareholders, and reinvests all its profit into the rail network. Its board comprises 'members' appointed from the rail industry and from users. It is subject to a regulatory agency, the Office of Rail Regulation (ORR), and it is underwritten by the government. Provision of rail *services* remains privatized, though on only a few busy lines has this produced choice for passengers.

The weakness of markets in these monopoly privatizations has been recognized by governments through the establishment of offices for public regulation of the service concerned. Regulation as such is a classic 'old' public service response to market failure, but modern regulatory procedures are based on sophisticated economic modelling, trying to reproduce the outcomes of a true market had it existed rather than on the implementation of bureaucratic rules. Privatization is therefore typically not a case of 'back to the market', but an attempt at providing a new compromise between markets and regulation, with private ownership and a form of regulation based on market principles, but with a continuing strong role for government agencies.

The users of these privatized services rarely notice much change in their status. Governments typically place contracts for the provision of a service with monopoly private providers, consumers using them just as they had used traditional monopoly public services: the 'customer' is the government, not the ultimate users. If we can assume that one of government's concerns in making contracts is to make good bargains, citizens as taxpayers may be considered to benefit, as costs and, therefore, their tax implications will be lower. But citizens as consumers may not gain at all, and may find that what makes a convenient contract for a large corporation and a central government department does not match their preferences. In particular, there will be a tendency for service delivery to take place in large, centralized form rather than locally, close to users. Of course, and as the Chicago school would remind us, this centralization will have achieved efficiencies, which will have increased overall wealth and therefore consumer welfare. If consumers then argue that they preferred local, if slightly less streamlined, services, they can be told that they do not understand what is in their own best interests. However, since they are not part of the market relationship between government and contracting firm, and since, according to neoliberals, there should be no politics involved in service provision, consumers will not in fact be asked for their opinions at all.

An example of this may be found in the policy adopted by the UK government in 2008 of encouraging the grouping of general medical practitioners (GPs) into large centres or 'polyclinics' in a small number of locations, rather than being scattered around a city. For some serious illnesses, medical practices more like small hospitals may be necessary. But for the great bulk of GPs' work, which concerns minor ailments of elderly and poor people and parents with small children, proximity of the service to patients' homes, avoiding the need for long journeys, is a highly appreciated feature of British medical service delivery. It predated the National Health Service, but interestingly was never abandoned during the classic period of that service's history, even though that regime is usually caricatured by marketization advocates as one of centralized command and control. Large centralized practices are, however, the mode of GP service delivery preferred by privately owned health delivery firms. Unsurprisingly, private firms have been winning most contracts for running these clinics, leaving existing groups of NHS GPs unable to compete. The UK government has been very concerned to 'make a market' in health services, and has consulted firms over what forms of organization would attract them into healthcare provision.

Private Providers Compete With Public, But Within Publicly Funded System

Solution (ii) in Table 4.2 is restricted to competition among public providers (as in choice of schools and hospitals among those provided by a public authority), and is not therefore our concern here, but in a more radical version private providers have been invited to compete with existing public ones. This introduction of an element of privatization may bring new capital to the disposal of the public service in question, and may also bring new ideas for delivery of the service. Initially, privatization programmes were seen as being limited to manufacturing industries, utilities and some of the smaller welfare services that did not attract political attention. By the late 1990s this had changed in many countries, and governments adopted a strategy of enabling customer choice via marketization within public services.

Again, the UK Labour governments of 1997–2010 and their Conservative/Liberal Democrat successor have been associated with the most radical steps. By the early twenty-first century the Labour Party had abandoned the belief that some services required public provision. This belief had been based on the assumption that there was such a thing as a public service professional ethic that supplied a better motive to providers of such things as healthcare than the maximization of profits. Like politicians in some other parties, Labour leaders came to interpret inadequacies of public services as being the fault of the staff working in them, in particular professionals. For right-of-centre parties, more naturally attracted to neoliberal solutions, public employees were always suspect, as they worked without the incentives of the market that should guarantee sensitivity to customers' preferences. Parties of the centre left were more likely to see public employees as their own constituency, but also had traditions of mistrusting relatively well-off professional elites, who were seen as having contempt for their clients. According to a leading social policy expert who became the British Labour Prime Minister's health policy adviser, Julian Le Grand (2006), the old model of the professions required the public to believe that all practitioners were 'knights', who could be trusted to work to the best of their abilities because of their professional commitment. But, he argued, few people were thoroughgoing knights. It was better to err on the side of caution and treat everyone as potential 'knaves', who would behave well only when given a financial market incentive to do so. Acceptance of this idea necessitated establishing market relationships between providers and their customers wherever possible, replacing reliance on professional ethics.

Professional ethics are not the same as public service ethics. Historically, the former partly developed in services provided privately, though with a protection from market forces afforded by associational and legal rules that limited competition. There has been continuing debate over whether these limitations protected clients from sharp practices that might be developed by profit-maximizing professionals (e.g. medical practitioners and dentists insisting on unnecessary treatments in order to make money out of a patient), or enabled professionals to charge high fees and treat clients contemptuously. The growth of the welfare state brought several professional services – mainly those in education and health – into the public sector for the mass of the population, joining some that were already in state service: the civil service, the military and, rather differently, the church. The concept of a combined professional public service ethos gradually emerged during the second part of the twentieth century. This became seen by many shades of political opinion, but especially the centre left, as a source of motivation that was an alternative to, perhaps superior to, the profit maximization of the private sector. This assumption was challenged by Le Grand and other neoliberal policy experts.

Acceptance of the Le Grand doctrine that it was better to suspect people of being knaves than to trust them to be knights led necessarily to preference for the profit motive over any so-called ethical basis for conduct. For Le Grand himself the main application of the approach was in the establishment of internal markets and consumer choice within publicly provided service. But it also led government logically to favour private providers, where the profit motive existed already.

Markets could only be made in policy fields where they had not previously existed if firms could be encouraged to enter them. Local education authorities were permitted to bid to build new schools only if no private contractors wanted to do so. Within the health service, local trusts were required to seek competitive bids from new producers to rival the services being offered by established local practitioners. This government also worked closely with US and other health service firms, seeking to learn what would encourage them to set up business within the NHS. In a further move, the 'New Models' programme gave public authorities incentives to give details of their work to private firms, in order to enable the latter to bid for contracts to take the work away from the authorities in question.

This kind of activity was justified by the need to 'make a market' where one had not existed before. In terms of relations between customer and supplier, it produced an odd concept of consumer 'sovereignty'. The government and other public agencies were, in effect, pleading with firms to 'please, accept us as your customers!'. It was the supplying corporations, not public services or their users, that gained from the establishment of markets constructed on these terms.

UK governments, and others following similar strategies, have until now maintained the policy that certain services should be free (or subject to nominal cost) at the point of receipt. In marketized public services (whether provided by public authorities or by private firms) users choose, and providers receive income as a result of their choice, but this is paid for by government, not by the user. This limits the extent to which users rather than government are the true 'customers'. There is also a problem that the universal service required by public health and education policy is not immediately attractive to private providers. An important element of any firm's strategy in the true market consists in finding niches: in the market it is not only customers who choose providers; also, providers choose customers. Firms often need inducements in terms of generous and long-lasting contracts if they are to manage without this important component of entrepreneurship. Indeed, long contracts are often justified. It would not be feasible to change the identity of the firm that organizes educational services or prisons in an area every year or so.

But the fact remains that contracts to provide services, demand for which is completely guaranteed for several years by government, give firms a highly attractive sellers' market. At a time when markets in general are becoming increasingly competitive on a global basis, public contracts have major attractions for firms. This also explains the strong pressure being exerted by representatives of private business on governments and international organizations to encourage privatization of public services. This has been so successful that the European Union (EU) and the World Bank, among other international institutions, now try to insist that governments must open their public services to private profit-making providers.

British governments responded enthusiastically to this by establishing public–private partnerships (PPPs), known in the UK as the Private Finance Initiative (PFI). An important motive of a government for doing this has been to fund building projects that it regards as important, such as new schools and hospitals, without distorting its budget by raising taxes or increasing government borrowing. The private sector finances the project, and therefore owns the facilities. In theory, the firm also takes over the risks involved in handling the capital, though in the UK following the financial crisis of 2008–9 government had to under-write the financial risks of its PFI contracts, so anxious was it that, otherwise, firms would lose interest in PFI deals. ('Please, accept us as your customers!')

A PFI firm leases the resource back to the public sector for a sum to be repaid over a period of years. During this period the project is managed jointly by the firm and the public service concerned. There is, however, a major rigidity here. If, say, a school or hospital is being funded within a PFI project, it is very difficult for the public authority concerned to change its use or the organizational arrangements surrounding it for 20 or sometimes 30 years, because the original uses tend to be enshrined in the initial contract.

The 'market' has operated at the single moment of establishing the contract; there is then an inflexible private monopoly, freed from market forces, for a lengthy period.

As in many privatizations, long PFI contracts bring in private firms while limiting the role of the market, again demonstrating how the neoliberal policy shift is more about firms than about markets. A contracting authority loses its chance to exercise a customer's power for the duration of the contract, and there is not necessarily any element of market choice for the ultimate consumer or service user. The subcontractor's customer is the public authority placing the contract. The subcontractor has no market relationship to the users, while the public also loses its 'citizenship' claims on the public authority, which is no longer responsible for the details of service provision. In some cases, where a lengthy chain of sub- and sub-subcontractors develops, any responsiveness to the user becomes a matter for lawyers for the various corporate partners to the contracts. This problem came to light during the first stage of the privatization of British railways, when, following a train crash that seemed to be related to poor track maintenance, it was difficult to find where, in a chain of contracts, responsibility lay.

Contract length removes day-to-day service provision from the discipline of the market, because the market exists only at the point of contract negotiation. One consequence of this has been the emergence of a group of firms that have expanded their businesses to cover a wide range of public services. For example, firms that started as road-building contractors (where customers are almost entirely public authorities) have become providers of administrative support services to local government. The core business of these enterprises is winning government contracts, almost irrespective of the substantive activities involved. Such firms achieve this position not just by learning how to bid and complete contract forms correctly, but by developing close relationships with government officials and politicians at national and local levels, which we shall consider below.

There is, however, a further, quite different, problem raised by these attempts to amalgamate private and public sector approaches to business. Where, as is usually the case with these arrangements, markets are highly imperfect, the service concerned is important to daily life and regulation continues to be required, the public continues to expect government to be involved somewhere in the service. According to neoliberal theory, this should not happen. Government and contractor stand in relationship to each other as principal and agent in a contract. At the outset the principal invites tenders from potential contractors for a task that is defined carefully in a tender document. Individual bidders may not receive insider information from the principal's representatives, nor may they learn what each other is bidding. On a formally determined date, the principal opens the bids. There may then be some detailed negotiations with a short list of bidders, until a decision is reached. Principals may also retain openly available lists of preferred contractors, on the basis of previous experience. These ensure that principals and contractors may benefit from learning from that experience, but such lists need to be subject to periodic revision to ensure that they have not become lists of 'cronies'. Finally, the principal specifies all that it wants done in the contract, and the agent discharges the contract in exchange for a specified fee. The contract may provide opportunities for revision, but these will be at specified points and will be formally defined.

The reason why contracts ideally take this form is that it ensures that no corruption takes place, which might happen were the principals' representatives to develop privileged relationships with certain contractors. It also ensures a high degree of access to the market, with a variety of contractors able to bid, and commits successful contractors to the terms that they offered and accepted when they won the contract. Any closer, continuing or informal communications between the representatives of principals and agencies compromise this position. Still speaking in ideal terms, these rules should govern contracting in the private sector, but they are regarded as essential in the public sector. If a private firm prefers to work with cronies and allow its staff to develop cosy relations with a few contractors, it will become inefficient and eventually be punished by the market; the public sector is not subject to this market test, so cosy and even corrupt contracting behaviour might continue indefinitely.

The problem with these ideal rules is that they do not work in the private sector, not just because corruption sometimes occurs, but for good reasons that we shall examine. If a similar relaxation is *not* permitted in the public sector, then that sector is debarred from using techniques that firms have discovered in order to avoid the rigidities of the formal contract model. If a similar relaxation *is* permitted, the corruption risks become real.

The problem with the formal contract model is that it cannot cope with the need for frequent adjustment and the implied terms that are intrinsic to any complex task. It is not possible to specify in advance in a contract all the problems and unexpected issues that arise in practice. In his studies of this phenomenon described in the previous chapter, Oliver Williamson found that principals' and agents' representatives working on complex tasks formed little cooperating units by themselves, often forgetting that in theory they worked for different sides of a contract, and ensured that they got the job done, even if this meant shifting the original terms to a limited extent.

This clearly also happens when the government is the principal and a private firm is the agent. A firm contracts, say, to run for several years a rail service previously in public ownership. There is necessarily intensive interaction between the staff of the firm and the staff of the ministry concerned – or, more likely, the regulatory agency established to monitor the railways. There may well be clear efficiency gains from this process. However, when government or a public agency is one of the parties, the adjustments that are made to the contract are not subject to the strict profitability test that a private firm is likely to apply. Further, the adjustments that take place are not to the original plans of one private firm at the suggestion of a contractor which is another private firm; they are changes in public policy made by a private firm.

The implied terms of contracts raise somewhat different issues. An agent brings to a contract not only the priced and itemized activities that reflect its own place within the market, but also any externalities from which it benefits. For example, a contracting firm may be linked to a local network of highly performing firms, which benefit from exchanges of tacit knowledge with each other. The principal party benefits from this network, although it did not ask for it. Now, these network effects do appear *implicitly* in the contract, as they contributed to the value for money that the contractor was able to offer and which gained the contract. However, given that implied terms are, by definition, not explicitly examined, how can the principal evaluate whether the value for money they promise is substantive or illusory? In the case of a networked firm we might be confident that the value for money is real. But what if the externality from which the contractor was benefiting was simply its past experience in knowing how to win contracts? What if its externality was not an ability to offer a good substantive deal, but such things as how to treat (perhaps literally) the principal's representatives, or, more innocently, simply experience in how to draft contracts cleverly? The core business of these enterprises is winning government contracts, almost irrespective of the substantive activities involved. Such skills may help a firm win a contract without offering anything in terms of improved service. Again, this can and no doubt does happen in purely private sector contracts. Where the principal is a part of government the risks are stronger because of the absence of a market check.

This brings us finally to the third weakness of public service identified by the neoliberal critique: item C in Table 4.2, its being out of touch with business.

Remoteness from the Private Sector

In classic public service traditions, it was necessary to maintain an arm's-length relationship between public officials and private firms. This was designed partly to protect markets

from political or administrative distortions through interventions designed to help 'friendly' firms, and at the extreme
to prevent actual corruption. It is in fact a concept closely
associated with a belief in free markets: if markets are to
function properly, there must be an absence of mutual interference between personnel in governments and private firms.
However, one of its consequences is considered to have been
that public service became cut off from developments in the
private sector, where competitive pressures lead to constant
innovation in ways of working. Governments have responded
to this in two main ways.

First, public bodies have been increasingly urged to behave
as though they were firms acting in the market. This is
encouraged by many of the practices listed in Table 4.2, such
as internal markets, the introduction of competition among
units and, most commonly, by the adoption of performance
targets for public service organizations and employees. It
also included the assertion of the model of principal (political leadership) and agent (public service top management),
taken from the neoliberal concept of the firm, in which the
principal (the shareholders) requires the agent (top corporate
management) to maximize share values. There is a problem
of finding a public service analogy for the maximization of
shareholder value. If politicians are the principals, then their
maximization strategy is aimed at electoral success; put sim-
plistically, therefore, 'votes' are the equivalent of shareholder
value. But democracy does not operate like profit, providing
a single measurable indicator. It constantly has to be inter-
preted by politicians, their advisers and other public opinion-
makers. In the end, therefore, the ethics of professions and
public service are displaced not by the market, but by the
ethics of politicians and, increasingly, by their private sector
management consultants.

This raises a highly important question: many marketization strategies in public policy try to put issues beyond
the range of conflict and debate, and beyond the reach of
difficult ethical choices. But these attempts must always
fail, as it is not possible to put human life on a technocratic

automatic pilot. It may be possible, within the corporate sector, for a chain of questions asking 'why do we do this?' to stop with the answer 'because it maximizes profit'. But that cannot dispose of the question from wider debate. As things stand in the early twenty-first century, such questions seem to find a final 'the buck stops here' resting place in the polity. It is very difficult for governments or the political class in general to foreclose principled debate. And this in turn limits their ability to imitate private business. But one can understand why politicians would dearly like to do so, and why they have been so very keen to try.

Second, and more central to our concerns, has been the encouragement of intensive interaction between public servants and private sector personnel, in order to enable the former to learn from the latter. In the process, the earlier idea of the need for a protective layer between public servants and private business people has been discarded. Private sector consultants have been taken deeply into government, not only offering advice but designing policies, and being able to recommend their own products for purchase. This has, for example, often happened with government purchase of a number of computer systems. Staff members from US health firms were appointed to advisory posts in the UK Department of Health in order to assist in the construction of a role for private firms in health provision, as discussed above. By the same token, the reverse process has also been encouraged, of politicians and civil servants leaving public office to work as consultants to private firms, using their contacts to help them win contracts.

Again in the UK, earlier rules preventing public officials from doing this until a lengthy period had elapsed have been relaxed, precisely in order to facilitate contacts between the public sector and private expertise. For example, Patricia Hewitt, a former Secretary of State for Health in the UK, took up two paid consultancy appointments soon after leaving office. One was with Boots, a major chain of pharmacies which was planning to develop GP services in its stores. The other was with Cinven, a private equity firm which had recently acquired a number of private hospitals. John Reid, a former Home Secretary with responsibility for security services, subsequently became a consultant to security firms running and bidding for government contracts.

The relationship between these developments and marketization is paradoxical. On the one hand, by seeking advice from individuals and organizations in the private sector, government is trying to get close to market-oriented forms of behaviour. On the other hand, by so doing it runs the risk of weakening the market. Too close a relationship between public officials and individual enterprises, leading to the construction of entry barriers around a privileged group of insider firms, results in the exclusion of others. Probably the biggest example of this to date was the subcontracting of many military and oil exploitation activities to private firms by the US administration of George W. Bush in its wars in Afghanistan and Iraq. Partly because of claims to needs for secrecy in such a context, many of these large contracts were awarded without a competitive bidding process. Prominent among the firms involved was Halliburton, of which the vice-president of the USA, Richard Cheney, had been chairman and CEO. Another, Blackwater, a military services corporation that derives over 90 per cent of its income from US government contracts, was eventually banned from Iraq by the Iraqi government following allegations of serious misconduct and corrupt practices. The firm has now changed its name to Xe.

We return to the fundamental dilemma of neoliberal strategy: in its attempt to reduce certain kinds of government intervention in the economy, it encourages or provides space for a number of mutual interferences between government and private firms, many of which raise serious problems for both the free market and the probity of public institutions.

Conclusion

The discussion in this chapter leaves us with three disturbing conclusions. First, although the neoliberal critique did identify genuine problems with classic public service, its remedies have sometimes turned out to be no better than the disease. For example, many marketization and privatization strategies have as one of their goals a reduction in the power of the public service professions. But the consequence has often been an increase in the power of private contractors.

We can usefully learn from this experience of privatization to be suspicious of all purveyors of panaceas – of those trying to 'sell' us the market as much as of an earlier generation of socialists who tried to tell us that state ownership of the economy would liberate us from human evil. It is understandable that politicians and their advisers would like to find simple, blanket approaches that they can apply to case after case, an internally consistent repertoire of policies to use whenever a new issue arises for which they have not been able to prepare. And this is something that they often feel they need above all else in their complex and hazardous task. But these blanket approaches, of whatever kind, are likely to provide robust answers only some of the time, because all policy repertoires come with characteristic weaknesses or failures.

The second conclusion relates to the core theme of this book: the uncomfortable role that the corporation is playing in the polity. Political debate concentrates on 'state versus market'; if the firm is considered, it tends to be assimilated, by supporters and critics alike, to the market. But we have now seen how that is not the case; the market does not always require the firm, and vice versa. In a further step, we have seen how neoliberalism fails to give an account of the firm, except for the unsatisfactory Chicago approach to anti-trust that we considered in the previous chapter. Just as this approach used the phrase 'consumer welfare' to disguise advocacy for corporations, so the idea of public service markets is being used for a process in which the gains to service users are not always clear, but those for subcontracting firms seem unambiguous. A full-blooded neoliberal approach to public services would have these moved fully into the market, with consumers paying for them themselves and government having no role at all. This has proved impossible, mainly for democratic reasons: the majority of voters will not support the abolition of the public services established during the heyday of universal suffrage. There is, however, a further factor, almost never discussed. Universal public services, funded by government rather than by individual consumer choice, provide wonderfully secure markets for those firms that specialize in contracting for public business. In the USA President Obama's health reforms were transformed, partly, into compulsory, partly subsidized, payments into corporate health insurance schemes. That was only one example among many.

Neoliberalism departs astonishingly from both the political and economic legacy of liberalism in not seeing any problem in a close relationship between firms and the state, provided the influence runs from firms to the state and not vice versa. The first error of this position is not to realize that firms try to influence the state precisely because they then want that influence to turn back onto the economy, to grant them favours.

When neoliberals do draw critical attention to uncomfortably close, competition-inhibiting relations between government and individual firms, it is because they have seen an ostensibly easy remedy: the complete disengagement of the state. According to pure neoliberal doctrine, there would be no worries about an unhealthy relationship between government and firms because government would not be involved in the firms' affairs. Every step towards regulation is an invitation to such a relationship. However, it is not only regulation but also deregulation, or abstention from regulation, that can produce inappropriate relations between firms and governments. The deregulation agenda that led to the irresponsible development of financial markets during the 1990s was itself the result of impressive lobbying in the US Congress and administration by banking interests. The abstention by government from involvement in health service provision in the USA, which distinguishes that country from the great majority of advanced democracies, is also the result of an extraordinary level of resources being deployed to lobby those same institutions.

Finally, all except the most extreme neoliberals accept that market efficiency does not account for the sum total of human objectives, and that a democracy has a right to establish alternative goals and parameters. But that process seems always to involve a government in intervening in what would otherwise be exclusively market behaviour. It is difficult to find institutions apart from the state that can deal with major externalities and public and merit goods. Government will therefore always be engaging in territory occupied, or potentially occupied, by private firms; and firms in turn must always be expected to deploy the resources they have won in the economy in order to intervene in the polity, so as to secure outcomes favourable to their economic activities. The move away from a state that provides services directly to one that subcontracts to private firms only serves to increase very considerably the scope for dubious interactions of this kind.

In Chapter 6 we shall confront the issues posed for democracy by the politically active corporation. But first, in Chapter 5, we must consider another, quite different, way in which the neoliberal alternative to government action has run into major difficulties in serving a public interest, but has done very well for certain corporate ones: housing finance and the secondary financial markets.

5

Privatized Keynesianism: Debt in Place of Discipline

Although overall the financial crisis of 2008–9, briefly discussed in Chapter 1, can be seen as a gigantic market failure, it can also be argued that it occurred precisely because some elements of the market model were becoming more and more perfect, in a way that damaged others. The process worked as follows. One of the biggest problems facing economic enterprises is uncertainty, the danger that something unforeseen will wreck business plans. But the market has an answer to this. For many forms of uncertainty one can make calculations of the odds that the worst will happen. Once one has done that, one can measure the probabilities associated with the uncertainty and calculate it in money terms, translating the uncertainty into calculable risk. At this stage it becomes possible to decide how much it is worth to accept the risk. This is the general principle of insurance. It then becomes possible to buy and sell these risks. Traders amass complex portfolios of different risks, planning to make a profit by succeeding in taking on more risks that turn out to be successful than those where the worst happens. This is a form of market activity that is essential to any innovatory and entrepreneurial activity; without it we would all be poorer.

The next step is that risk traders do not wait to see if their bet actually materializes, but sell the risk they have bought to another trader. Their calculation does not so much concern the actual risk of the loan, but how much they can get for it in the secondary market. This price will depend on what the trader believes that likely purchasers of the risk will believe that the risk is worth. This will of course be based on the calculation of the original risk, but it will be slightly distorted by the fact that it is the first trader's belief about what potential second traders will believe about the risk that forms the basis of the calculation, rather than the first trader's beliefs about the risk as such. In itself, this secondary trading is also benign, as, by spreading risks widely, it reduces the exposure of any one risk bearer.

From the late 1980s onwards these secondary markets in risk were developing very rapidly into extended chains of trading. The second trader in the chain would be willing to buy the risk for a price based on what he believed a third trader would pay for it; the third trader would buy the risk for a price based on what he believed a fourth trader would pay, and so on, with a slight increase in distortion at every point. Two factors led to these chains becoming extremely long indeed. First, the globalization of the economy meant that wealth holders in more and more countries could engage in risk-trading markets. This was an expanding universe. As a result, the amount of risk for which any one participant in a trade was responsible was reducing as more actors appeared to share the risk. This also seemed benign.

Second, led by the US and UK governments pursuing the general neoliberal agenda, regulations governing financial transactions were being relaxed across most parts of the world. An important legislative change in the USA in 1999, the Gramm-Leach-Bliley Financial Services Modernization Act, a fundamental part of the neoliberal deregulation programme, abolished long-standing restraints on the ability of retail banks to use their customers' deposits for high-risk trading activities. These restraints had been introduced in 1933 in the Glass-Steagall Act in the immediate wake of the

1929 Wall Street crash. Repeal of Glass-Steagall gave high-risk traders access to the savings of millions of people, who were themselves unaware of what was going on. That was not so benign.

Risks were being traded at increasing velocity, increasing the chain of 'beliefs about beliefs' that, slightly each time, was gradually distancing the prices in the market from evaluations of the original risks. These distortions would not have mattered if they were just the result of differences in individual estimates, as optimistic evaluations of risk might have been cancelled out by pessimistic ones and vice versa. There was, however, a prevailing mood of optimism: the system was constantly growing, distributing risks more widely. Also – and this was to prove fundamental – the system was becoming so vast and involving such a high proportion of the world's wealth that, if the worst came to the worst and the risks at stake proved to be far higher than anyone anticipated, governments around the world would simply have to step in and save the system. In a further step, banks constructed bundles of very varied risks, in which quite safe loans were mixed up with unsecured mortgages in unspecified proportions, but the traders buying them showed no interest in examining the bundles, as they were geared solely to the set of beliefs about sets of beliefs about sets of beliefs in an almost infinite regress that was setting prices in the secondary markets.

In such a system money is made through the velocity of transactions. Every time one sells a risk for slightly more than one paid for it, one makes a profit; buy another risk with the proceeds and sell it quickly, and even more money will be made. Traders working for the banks and permitted to use the savings and investments of millions of customers in order to play these markets were themselves paid bonuses related to their performance. The faster the traders could buy and sell, the higher these bonuses would be. Their incentives led them to concentrate on shorter and shorter time horizons.

Prices in the secondary markets became considerably more important than original evaluations of the risks. It was then successfully argued that the evaluations being made in these secondary markets could replace any attempt at estimating the value of assets in their primary markets, as the secondary markets had become the more important reality. It ceased to make sense to ask if the bets being placed in the secondary markets reflected underlying 'real' values; the secondary values *were* the real values. It was like betting at a race-track where no horses ever run, bets reflecting only estimates of what other gamblers might be betting. Eventually, ratings agencies – firms that in theory are paid to evaluate the risk-worthiness of banks or even national economies – started to base their ratings on the secondary markets themselves, even though in theory a credit rating should provide a different and independent assessment of risk-worthiness. Finally, even corporate accounting systems were changed, so that instead of estimating the values of the assets of a firm in terms of the value of its labour, capital, markets, etc., accountants looked simply at the stock market value of these assets, a value formed by traders' beliefs about other traders' beliefs, etc.

At one level this was the most perfect expression of the power of markets that the world had ever seen. Calculations of the value of a firm's assets, or of the size of a risk, were being set by some very pure markets rather than by arbitrary human judgements; and the vast sharing of risk that was developing enabled many important risk-taking ventures to be funded in the 'real' economy. The purchasing power of many millions of people was enhanced. At another level, however, these same perfect market processes were destroying certain other essential components of a well-functioning market, rather in the way that in certain wasting diseases some organs function hyperactively and destroy others in the process. If we look back over the above discussion, we note, first, that traders were being given incentives to ignore information, as attention was diverted from what risks might be worth in primary markets to what they were in the secondary ones. Second, the system encouraged excessive optimism.

Stock markets have always been vulnerable to fashion and mood swings: if a particular asset is seen as likely to be profitable, everyone wants to buy it; if a rumour unsettles that view, everyone wants to sell. Over time, the market corrects itself, but for lengthy periods before such correction takes place, prices can become very distorted, leading to abrupt and serious shocks when the correction takes place. The market is supposed to smooth distortions gradually, as rational actors adapt to a changing situation; but rushes to participate in booms and avoid slumps impose a different logic of action. The history of financial markets is not one of long-standing smooth adjustments, but of successive crises. To look back only over the decade that preceded the 2008–9 crisis, there had been the vast Asian debt crisis of 1997–8, the dot.com bubble of 1999–2000, and the Argentinian crisis of 2002.

Third, an important element in the excessive optimism was confidence among traders – a confidence that proved to be justified – that governments would not let the system fail and would therefore move in to compensate them for any losses they made through excessive trading. As Martin Wolf commented in the *Financial Times* (see also his book *Fixing Global Finance*, 2008), the banks learned how to privatize gain and socialize loss. While things were going well, they could engage in wildly optimistic trading, earning high profits; if things suddenly went wrong, governments would come to the rescue. Looking towards the future, the banks now know for certain that governments will bail them out and will be willing later to make cuts in public services in order to finance the rescue operation. As a result, they will now take higher risks than before. The one major attempt by a government to refuse to accept this implicit blackmail – the US government's willingness to allow Lehman Brothers to collapse – produced such a shock reaction in the markets that after that there were just offers of open-handed rescue. As the banks make their future risk calculations, this renewed confidence in government rescue will enable them to play for even higher stakes than in the past. Bankers' rewards are justified by the argument that because they create profits, they create wealth, and that we all benefit from an increase in wealth. But these profits are made possible only by the support of government, which, not being part of the profit-making economy, is written off as not being wealth-creating. Therefore neither it nor its taxpayers are to be compensated for the enormous sums that they have paid to the banks to help them escape the consequences that a true free market would have imposed upon them.

A fourth implication of the system casts doubt on the claim that the risk-sharing model was favourable to innovation and enterprise. Firms in the real economy – that is, making goods and providing services for sale to customers who use them as such rather than buying them in order to trade in them – need time and money to bring new projects to fruition. It takes time to develop a new idea, evaluate its chances in the market, bring to bear the investment to produce it, and then sell it to customers. There will be a time lag during which the firm's managers need the shareholders to wait, holding off reaping a dividend in the expectation that a successful product will bring them a good return. Their willingness to do this may well be dependent on the existence of a lively share market that will enable them quickly to get out of a firm if there are signs that the new product will not succeed; there would be a major disincentive to risk-taking if they felt they had no escape. Share markets are not therefore necessarily the enemies of innovation. However, developments in the secondary markets during the early twenty-first century reached a point where shareholders were interested solely in trading share values in these markets – which, as we have seen, were based on extremely short-term calculations of gain dependent on beliefs about beliefs about beliefs increasingly remote from projects in the real economy. In the most sophisticated developments, banks have developed information technologies that enable shares to be bought and sold during fractions of a second, in a purely computer-driven process.

Implications for the Shareholder Model

The rise of the finance-driven form of capitalism described above is linked to the Anglo-American shareholder maximization concept of the firm. This concept does not *require* the idea of secondary risk markets, but the historical appearance of the two together has had important consequences. Under the shareholder maximization model the sole goal of a corporation is to maximize value for shareholders; all other interests are not so much subordinate to that as deemed to be incorporated within it. This idea might seem to contradict the slogan that in a capitalist economy 'the customer is king'. How can customers and shareholders both be sovereign? The argument works as follows. In a perfectly competitive market, firms can maximize their shareholders' value only if they are satisfying customers, as a firm that disappoints its customer will lose business to rivals that are putting the customer first; as a result the first firm's shareholders would see sub-optimal performance. Therefore the maximization of shareholder value also ensures consumer sovereignty. If the market is not perfect – if, for example, firms are able to take advantage of customers' difficulty in acquiring adequate information about products – then Chicago economics has the alternative answer that we have already considered: maximizing shareholder value maximizes the overall wealth in the society, and this is deemed to be identical with consumer welfare.

Shareholder maximization is not the only approach to corporate governance to be experienced by modern capitalism. French, German and Japanese capitalism, for example, all developed with concepts of a diversity of stakeholders to whom a firm owed responsibility, directly and not en route to looking after shareholder value: customers, employees, bond-holders, sometimes local communities or a national interest. These models were generally pushed aside during the 1990s, as the Anglo-American model asserted its superiority as the most perfect expression of neoliberal ideals. This superiority was partly based on what seemed at the time to have been the better economic performance of the UK and

US economies – a performance which we now know was being borne along by the discredited risk-trading approach. More substantively, the stakeholder economies depended on local understandings and shared experiences that embedded firms in their societies and enabled people in those societies (rightly or wrongly) to trust the juggling of different interests that the model recognized. The shareholder model was more consistent with the anonymous global economy, where it is both necessary and possible to deal with strangers, without embeddedness and with no need for personal trust. Under the Anglo-American model, it is necessary only to trust that the market is a pure one. Stakeholder models proved to be local and incapable of export compared with this. The shareholder maximization model triumphed, and with it the idea that maximizing shareholders' gain would ensure that other interests were satisfied.

In the history of US capitalism the rise of the shareholder model had been a response to a previous period known as that of managerial capitalism. From the 1930s onwards, and in the wake of the great crash of 1929, the US economy came to be dominated by large, complex corporations. Shareholders – in those days, mainly groups of wealthy but not necessarily well-informed families – did not understand much about the businesses in which they held shares, and therefore usually deferred to senior managers. These were then suspected of building up large organizations in the interests of their own salaries and egos. By the 1970s economic theorists had posed what they called the 'principal–agent problem': under what circumstances could a principal (i.e., the body of shareholders) trust their agents (senior managers) not to pursue their own interests at the expense of the owners? The answer was deemed to lie in reforms of corporate governance that placed the shareholders' interests at the peak. In fact, an Anglo-American corporation is nothing more in law than a bundle of shares – unlike, for example, a German corporation, which is seen in law as 'belonging' to the wider range of stakeholders.

An example of how this approach can affect the way in which corporations work can be seen in a well-known contribution to debate by Michael Jensen (2001), a professor at the Harvard Business School and one of the leading advocates of the shareholder maximization concept. Like many neoclassical economists, Jensen was perplexed by the rise of corporate social responsibility. This concept, which we shall encounter in more detail in the next chapter, concerns the voluntary acceptance by firms of obligations to customers, workers and, in particular, the wider community, going beyond their market activities. Decisions about such policies are normally taken by senior managers, and they might be considered to compromise profit maximization. Imagine, for example, a multinational clothing corporation that subcontracts its production of garments to countries in the Far East where young children are employed to work long hours in the factories with no pressure from national or local government to prevent it. Assume that senior managers in the corporation are revolted by this and decide not to allow their suppliers to employ child labour. This will bring the prices of their T-shirts and jeans above the levels of their rivals, who are happily still using child labour. Assuming that these products are competing mainly on price, the corporation will see a decline in its sales and therefore its profits. From Jensen's perspective and from that of principal–agent theory in general, the managers have betrayed their duties to their principals. Also, since it is an axiomatic assumption of economic theory that consumers have an overwhelming interest in low prices, the managers have betrayed their customers, whose interests are in any case identical to those of shareholders, according to Chicago doctrine.

But Jensen does not like the implication that flows from this, that firms must always be amoral actors. He therefore argues that it is necessary for someone (it is not clear who) to educate shareholders into accepting a moral approach to business. As the principals, shareholders are free to decide not to maximize profits in order to achieve some social good.

The problem of this argument is that it empowers property-owners alone with the capacity to be moral agents, at least within the sphere of the economy – and, as we have seen, it is part of neoliberal strategy to spread the economic approach to all parts of society, depriving us of any sphere where different values appear. The rest of us must perform as amoral automata, being only the agents of share-owning principals. Interestingly, the debate over this concerns the relative moral rights and duties of share-owners and senior managers. That everyone else working for the firms has no right to be a moral agent is taken for granted.

It must be remembered that when we speak of owners of giant firms in the contemporary economy we no longer refer to the idea of entrepreneur owners or even of institutional shareholders who maintain long-term relations with senior managers. Under shareholder value maximization, the role of owners is to look at share prices alone. Actual shareholders delegate their decision-making to traders acting for them who take interest only in the secondary market for a firm's shares – on the extreme velocity of which their own rewards depend. The powerful players in the financial markets do not 'hold' shares at all; they just trade them. The connection between ownership of a business and concern for even the financial aspects of its actual performance has become highly attenuated. And yet this shareholder interest remains the only legitimate interest in a corporation in the eyes of Anglo-American corporate law.

There is a further important consequence of the combination of shareholder maximization and highly active, short-term-oriented share markets. In theory, shareholders' earnings, their dividends, based on the profits, are the residuum in a firm's trading activities, the last claim that is made on a firm after all claims from bond-holders, employees, creditors, investment needs and other requirements have been met. This is the risk-bearing activity at the heart of capitalism that enables firms to be innovative and that justifies shareholder maximization: if shareholders must wait until all other contractual claims on a firm have been met, then they need to be able to have the final say over how the firm is managed. Also, their rewards from successful transactions must be high, as these must compensate them for losses that will come from risks that go wrong.

This principle remains valid if a firm goes bankrupt; shareholders have the last claims on any assets. But during routine operations of a viable company it has been heavily compromised by the emergence of profit expectations within today's highly volatile stock markets. Ideas spread as to what short-term return on profits ought to be available in the market; remember, shares are being bought and sold with an eye primarily on the secondary markets. There will therefore be a flight from shares of firms not meeting the prevailing idea of a good return. Such firms become vulnerable to hostile takeover, something which senior managers are keen to avoid, as it often leads to them losing their jobs. Managers are therefore under strong pressure to meet or exceed a target level of returns to shareholders. If necessary, investment plans, customer service and employee compensation will have to be held back to meet this target. Once this occurs, distributed profits are no longer a residuum, but are an early call on a firm's earnings. They are ceasing to be rewards for commercial risk, but are being protected from all risks other than those stemming from a collapse of secondary markets (where, we now know, government will protect them anyway).

Tracking down in detail the ways in which this shift in the role of shareholding is making firms fail to give customers a decent service would require very complex research with a difficult counterfactual task: we should have to discover what products and services customers would have been offered had competition for short-term capital not outweighed competition in the development of improved customer service in managers' calculations. Where product markets remain competitive despite these changes, firms will still have to please customers in order to please shareholders, and the problem will not arise; where markets are not competitive, no one will be producing the products or providing the services that might have been produced had share markets behaved differently. But we cannot study a might have been.

One very perceptible example of conflict of interest between shareholders and other stakeholders, which presents us very directly with the transfer of risk away from the former, concerns occupational and private pension schemes managed by profit-making corporations. Until the recent past, most pension schemes have been based on the principle of 'defined benefits'. Members of a pension fund pay stipulated contributions each month from their salary, and when they retire they receive a pension defined as a proportion of their salary during a stated period of years, usually their final ones in employment. It is the responsibility of the fund's actuaries to ensure that the contributions adequately finance the pensions. The risk that this might not work out is borne by the fund's shareholders on the usual principle that profit is the risk-bearing element of a firm's finances.

Large sums of money accumulate in pension funds, as the sums flowing in as contributions are larger than those being paid out as pensions. The fund uses this money to invest in various financial markets. These markets have become highly lucrative, as a result of the processes discussed above. This by-product of pension insurance activity, rather than the provision of pensions, became the primary business of pension funds, which have become among the world's biggest investors. The actual paying out of pensions therefore became burdensome to them, especially as increasing longevity was playing havoc with their actuarial calculations. Gradually, therefore, they have been closing their defined benefits schemes and moving towards 'defined contributions' schemes. Under these, members look forward to no predictable level of pension at all. The fund invests their contributions in the stock market, and on retirement a sum is allocated to pensioners corresponding to the stock market evaluation of their stock of contributions on that day. They may be lucky and retire during a stock market boom; they might retire during a slump. Whichever occurs determines their pension for the rest of their lives. The level of pensions thus becomes the risk-bearing residuum of the fund's activities, risk having been transferred away from shareholders, who, as the fund's principals, have been demanding guaranteed profit rates.

General Complicity in the Model

The description so far of how financial markets have developed under the shareholder maximization model implies a parasitical system that might easily be removed to general advantage. Unfortunately, matters are more complex than this. Many millions of people, including many on relatively low incomes, particularly in the Anglo-American world, have been nourished on crumbs from the rich man's table.

This happened through the relationship between growing home-ownership and the secondary markets. From the 1980s onwards growing proportions of people on modest incomes in many wealthy countries started buying their own homes through mortgage finance. This was not a pure market development; in several countries, particularly the UK and USA, governments encouraged the growth by relaxing the terms on which housing finance could be obtained, and by taking economic policy measures to ensure that house prices kept rising – essential to giving buyers confidence that they could take on the initially high loans involved in mortgages. Banks and other financial institutions could make these loans to customers who found it hard to afford them, because the rising value of the property meant that, in the event of a need to repossess, the bank would acquire an asset that had grown in value. In a further development, as property values rose, people could take on a higher mortgage, extending the pay-back period and gaining useful cash with which they could buy other products. At the same time credit card markets were growing, leading people to take on more debt at high interest rates in order to fund purchases. The general buoyancy of the economy was being sustained by debt.

In most societies and in most historical periods, debt has been concentrated among wealthier groups, who think of it as an investment, using their resources of property and other wealth as collateral for the loans. The past three decades have been distinctive for the spread of high debt levels to people on modest incomes and whose only wealth is a house that is heavily mortgaged.

While rising property values meant that the loans being made to these people were not wildly insecure, banks began to exploit the scope offered by these risks further by trading them on the secondary markets, subjecting them to the process of risk-sharing described above. In particular they would include tranches of unsecured mortgage and credit card debt in packages alongside less risky propositions in the bundles that were being traded, safe in the knowledge that purchasers would not look into the contents of the bundles, for the reasons we have described. In this way therefore the secondary markets, radically unstable as they were, 'helped' sustain high levels of consumption and therefore vibrant economies by enabling people on modest incomes to spend money that they did not have. In this way we all became complicit in the financial model, a fact that makes it even harder for governments to resist the demands of the banks that they be put back on their feet and allowed to start all over again.

Karl Marx considered that at certain moments of historical crisis a social class would emerge whose particular interests coincided with the general interest of society. Such classes triumphed in the revolutions in which the crises ended. Marx's error was to believe that when the class concerned became the international proletariat there would be an end to the process, because the proletariat was the generality of society and not just a particular interest within it. This was an error if only because it is impossible to imagine anything as vast as the global proletariat producing organizational forms that could express a shared interest. In reality the proletariat appeared on the stage of political history in national packages, oriented towards the political possibilities

presented by individual nation-states. Be that as it may, the
Keynesian model that guided economic policy in the first 30
years after the Second World War did represent a temporary
coincidence between the interests of the industrial working
class in the global northwest and a general interest of the
politico-economic system. This had been the class likely to
threaten political and social order. It was also potentially the
class whose mass consumption, if facilitated and made
secure, could fuel economic growth of a kind unprecedented
in human history. Finally, it was a class that had produced
political parties, trade unions and other organizations, as
well as associated intellectuals, to shape and press its
demands. The Keynesian model, combined with mass production, was a response to these demands that reconciled
workers with a capitalist system of production.

The opposing set of neoliberal ideas that leapt to prominence during the 1970s inflationary crisis of the Keynesian
model was also carried by a class: the class of finance capitalists, geographically grounded primarily in the USA and
the UK, but extending across the globe. Their transnational
character was a major advantage, as a further change that
was taking place was the declining autonomy of the nation-
state. The postwar political economy had been founded on
the basis of governments that could exercise considerable
discretion in how they managed their economies. By the
1980s the process generally known as globalization, both a
producer and a product of the deregulation of financial
markets, had eroded much of that autonomy. The only actors
capable of rapid action at global level were giant transnational corporations (TNCs), which preferred their own
private regulation over that by governments. This both
advanced and even rendered necessary the new model.

If the world was to gain from the liberation of productive
forces and enterprise that the spread of free markets would
bring, the class of those who dealt in the unregulated finance
that massaged and helped those markets to grow would
benefit particularly. Whereas the tight labour markets and
regulated capitalism of the Keynesian period had seen a

gradual reduction in inequalities of wealth in all advanced countries, the following period was to see a reversal of these trends, with the highest rewards going to those working in financial institutions.

Two questions are immediately raised by this history. First, what had been the fate of the industrial working class, whose interests had seemed so politically urgent in the 1940s and 1950s? And what became of the need to reconcile the instability of markets with people's demand for security in their lives, which had been both politically and economically so important?

The initial crisis of Keynesianism in the 1970s had been accompanied by an extraordinary wave of industrial militancy, such that one might have thought that the challenge of that class was becoming more rather than less central. But this was an illusion. Rising productivity and the globalization of production were in fact undermining its demographic base. Starting in the USA, the UK and Scandinavia, the share of employment in mining and manufacturing began to decline throughout the West. The militancy of the 1970s served only to encourage governments that were so inclined to lend their hand to hastening that decline, as occurred in the UK with reference to the coal and some other industries during the 1980s. Industrial workers had never constituted a majority of the working population anywhere, but they had been the growing class; now they were declining. By the 1980s they had been replaced as leaders in industrial militancy by public employees, with whom governments could deal directly without disturbing the market economy much. Workers in the main growth sectors of the new economy, private services, were usually not organized and had developed no autonomous political agenda, no organizations to articulate their specific grievances.

In the regime of largely unregulated international finance that was instituted during the 1980s, governments were far more worried about capital movements than about labour movements: positively, in that they wanted to attract investment from free-floating capital with short time horizons; negatively, in that they feared that such capital would move away if they did not provide conditions in which it was happy.

The matter was not quite that simple: the Keynesian model itself had met an economic demand from capitalists themselves for stable mass consumption as well as workers' demands for stable lives. In the newly industrializing countries of South Asia and the Far East this was not a problem, as the economies of these largely undemocratic countries have depended on exports and consumption by wealthy local elites. They have not needed spending by the mass of their populations. But this was far from possible in the existing advanced economies. Indeed, dependence there on increased domestic consumption rather than exports had intensified rather than weakened. As the industries making many of the products bought in mass markets moved to new producing countries, or, if they didn't move became dependent on less and less labour, employment growth came to depend on markets in personally delivered services, which are not so subject to globalization. It is easy to buy a Chinese T-shirt in a western shop and benefit from low Chinese wages; it is hardly feasible to travel to China to get a cheap haircut. Immigration is the main way that globalization affects such services, but its impact is limited by controls on population movements, and by the fact that immigrants' wages, though usually low, are not as low as those of the workers they have left behind in their home countries. So the puzzle remains: if the instability of free markets had initially been an obstacle to the development of the mass consumption economy, how did the latter survive the return of the former?

During the 1980s (or 1990s, depending on when the neo-liberal wave hit a particular economy) the answer first appeared to be that mass consumption would not survive, as rising unemployment and continuing recession became the dominant experience. Then things changed. By the end of the twentieth century the UK and the US, in particular, were demonstrating declining unemployment and strong growth. One explanation might be that in a really pure market economy, the rapid alternations of boom and bust associated with the earlier history of capitalism do not occur. In the perfect market there is perfect knowledge, rational actors can therefore perfectly anticipate what is going to happen, and can adapt their behaviour to produce a seamless web of adaptation. Did the USA and the UK really enter this nirvana at the turn of the century?

No. Knowledge remains far from perfect; exogenous shocks, whether hurricanes, wars or the actions of irrational people who do not behave as theory says they should, continue to impact on economies and to disturb calculations. We now know that two very different forces came together to rescue the neoliberal model from the instability that would otherwise have been its fate: the growth of credit markets for poor and middle-income people, and the emergence of derivatives and futures markets among the very wealthy. This combination produced a model of 'privatized Keynesianism' that occurred initially by chance, but which gradually became a crucial matter for public policy. Instead of governments taking on debt to stimulate the economy, individuals and families did so, including some rather poor ones.

This helps explain the great puzzle of the period: how did moderately paid American workers in particular, who have little legal security against instant dismissal from their jobs, and salaries that might remain static for several years, maintain consumer confidence, when continental European workers with more or less secure jobs and annually rising incomes were bringing their economies to a halt by their unwillingness to spend? US, British and Irish house prices were rising every year; the proportion of the value of the house on which a loan could be raised was also rising until it reached more than 100 per cent; credit card possibilities were growing. With some exceptions, continental European property values remained stable. Mortgage and credit card debt reached considerably higher levels in the Anglo-American economies than in typical continental European ones. One must recall that in Germany and some other

European economies the growth model had never become quite so dependent as the Anglo-American ones on domestic consumer spending. As a result, the export-oriented manufacturing sector had remained stronger; government policy was more concerned with keeping export prices low, and less concerned to maintain domestic consumption of locally produced services. In both types of economy public policy was bearing down on wages – in the Anglophone countries by reducing collective labour rights that might interfere with markets; in Germany and in some other European countries through the firm anti-inflationary stance of the European Central Bank. Continental European, Japanese and a wide range of new producing countries were dependent on US, and to a lesser extent UK, consumers buying their goods. But what would enable these consumers to do so? This is where the debt model became so important and ceases to be able to be written off as parasitical.

Anti-inflationary policy bears down on the prices of goods and services that lose their value as they are consumed. Producers of goods as well as services like restaurants or health centres confront an environment hostile to rises in their prices. This is not the case with assets, non-consumables that keep their value after purchase: real property, financial holdings, many art objects. A rise in their price is simultaneously a rise in their value, and does not contribute to inflation. Assets, and earnings based on assets, have, logically, not been the objects of neoliberal counter-inflation policy. Therefore, anything that could be switched from earnings derived from the sale of normal goods and services to an asset base has done very well under this policy regime. This has applied to proportions of salaries paid as share options and to spending funded by extended mortgages based on property values rather than by salaries and wages.

Eventually, governments began to incorporate privatized Keynesianism into their explicit public policy thinking, though the phrase did not occur to them. While a reduction in the price of oil would be seen as good news (because it reduced inflationary pressure), a reduction in the price of houses would be seen as a disaster (as it would undermine confidence in debt), and government would be expected to act through fiscal or other measures to get prices rising again. The UK government increasingly relaxed the constraints imposed on granting mortgages, while the two state-owned mortgage firms in the USA – Fannie Mae and Freddie Mac – played prominent parts in the sub-prime markets.

The dependence of the democratic capitalist system on rising wages, a welfare state and government demand management that had seemed essential for mass consumer confidence has been withering away. The bases of prosperity shifted from the social democratic formula of working classes supported by government intervention to the neoliberal conservative one of banks, stock exchanges and financial markets. Ordinary people played their part, not as workers seeking to improve their situation through trade unions, legislation protecting employment rights and publicly funded social insurance schemes, but as debt-holders, participants in credit markets. This fundamental political shift was more profound than anything that could be produced by alternations between nominally social democratic and neoliberal conservative parties in government as the result of elections. It has imparted a fundamental rightward shift to the whole political spectrum, as the collective and individual interests of everyone are tied to the financial markets, which in their own operations act highly unequally, producing extreme concentrations of wealth.

Behind the financial crisis we can recognize some familiar market failures: the failure of price to act as a signal of value; and deficiency of information. Rapid dealing in secondary markets uncoupled the prices of assets from the combinations of land, labour and capital that constitute the 'real' assets of a firm. In principle, share prices reflect a firm's commercial prospects, and therefore convey important and accurate information about the firm. Extended secondary markets in shares distorted that relationship. Financial entrepreneurs and accountancy firms developed forms of knowledge – of prices of bundles of assets that required no knowledge of what was contained in the bundles – that encouraged eventually self-destructive decisions. This was the Achilles heel of the model, corresponding to the inflationary ratchet of original Keynesianism.

Not surprisingly, when the secondary markets collapsed no one had any idea of exactly how much money had been lost or where it had gone. If the only information that counts is totally reflexive and cannot be validated outside itself, then information cannot play the role that the market needs it to play. But for so many years no one holding power within or over the system paid any attention to this, despite the strong warning that had been sounded only a few years before when the dot.com bubble burst at the end of the 1990s. Here too, asset values had become based on an almost infinite regress of expectations of value, gradually losing all touch with what the actual products of internet-based firms might be. Enthusiasts of that system had believed that they had discovered the Holy Grail of stock market prices that need never fall; the iron laws of supply and demand had apparently been broken without retribution. No learning on the basis of this experience appeared to inform behaviour in the financial system during the few years that intervened between these two similar crises.

Once privatized Keynesianism had become a model of general economic importance, it became a kind of bizarre collective good, however nested in private actions it was. Necessary to it was behaviour by banks that has to be defined as irresponsible, as it involved their not carrying out checks and accountancy practices that they were in principle assumed to do; but millions of people gained by buying real goods and services through the unreal money that was generated. Therefore *that very irresponsibility became a collective good*. There has been considerable discussion of the serious moral hazards involved in governments coming to the aid of banks which have suffered from this irresponsibility; but there is a far wider moral hazard involved in this complicity of virtually whole societies in the irresponsible practices in the first place. Historical theories of the market had always depicted its role as ensuring that the pursuit of selfish interests would take place in a manner that also secured collective and general ones. This was relaxed as neoliberalism became harnessed to the hedonistic mood of the wealthy classes of the 1980s and 1990s. But the link between private interests and collective good could not be completely severed, as economic behaviour is never of purely private interest. The relationship between private and collective therefore expressed itself in the curiously back-handed form of the link between irresponsible banking and general welfare.

Neoliberalism, compromised by the soft approach of Chicago economics towards concentrations of wealth in market-dominating corporations, and further compromised by having created, through banking deregulation, markets that thrive on inadequate information, has led us into a trap: we can secure our collective welfare only by enabling a very small number of individuals to become extremely rich and politically powerful. The essence of this trap is perfectly expressed in what is now happening to the welfare state. Governments have to make deep cuts in social services, health and education programmes, pension entitlements and social transfers to the poor and unemployed. They have to do this to satisfy the anxieties of the financial markets over the size of public debt, the operators in these markets being the very same people who benefited from the bank rescue, and who have already begun to pay themselves high bonuses – bonuses 'earned' because their operations have been guaranteed against risk by the government spending that created the public debt.

After Privatized Keynesianism:
The Responsible Corporation?

How will the enormous moral hazard established by governments' recognition of financial irresponsibility as a collective good now be managed? In addressing this question, it is necessary to start from acceptance that political and economic elites will do everything that they can to maintain neoliberalism in general and the finance-driven form of it in particular. They have benefited so much from the inequalities of wealth and power that the system has produced, compared with the experience of strongly redistributive taxation, strong trade unions and government regulation that constituted the so-called social democratic period. Those features had been tolerated because they seemed to be necessary to sustain mass consumption and to prevent industrial workers from becoming communists. Communism has now, fortunately, gone for ever, while the possibility of basing mass consumption on a system of massive private debt through the financial markets also happened to make some people very rich indeed. They will cling to this model tenaciously.

Economic prosperity continues to depend on supplies of capital through efficient markets far more than it previously depended on the industrial workers of the western world. A difference of geographical reach is part of the explanation. The decline of the western industrial working class does not mean a decline in that class globally. More people are engaged in manufacturing activities today than ever before; but they remain divided into national lumps with very different histories, cultures, levels of living, organized interests and trajectories. Finance capital does not come in such lumps, but is more like a liquid or gas, capable of changing shape and flowing across jurisdictions and regions. We remain dependent on both labour and capital, but the former is subject to *divide et impera*, the latter is not – unless we see a major return to economic nationalism and limitations on capital movements that would inflict major economic decline on us all.

The most likely new model is one that will depend increasingly on those corporations; the logic of globalization that imparted an important role to TNCs has not disappeared with the financial system. We arrive once again at the tension at the heart of neoliberalism: is it about markets or about giant firms?

The initial response of governments to the financial crisis has been a return to regulation and even temporary bank nationalization. However, this will not last. We can anticipate what will happen if we look back to what was, in retrospect, the first sign that the financial markets were not as effective at automatic self-regulation as had been claimed on their behalf: the Enron, WorldCom and other scandals discussed briefly in the previous chapter. In its response to these cases, the US Congress imposed tight regulations on company auditing in the Sarbanes-Oxley Act. This was passed by large majorities and even supported by President Bush, who had rapidly distanced himself from Enron, his erstwhile campaign donor. However, as soon as memories of the enormity of the crimes had started to fade, lobbyists for the finance industry began to complain that enterprise was being stifled, and to threaten that finance houses would leave New York for the more permissive regimes in London and elsewhere. The same process is already beginning again before the bout of regulatory measures visited on the financial sector as part of the deal with governments to save it has even been completed. How can the derivatives markets get to work in supporting high levels of borrowing if they are to be subject to rules that make much of that borrowing more difficult? How can traders fulfil their necessary task of recouping banks' losses unless they have incentives in the form of large bonuses? By 2010 nearly all the old practices in the secondary markets had re-established themselves. The corporate lobbyists set to work in the US Senate, heavily weakening President Obama's bill to tighten regulation on the sector.

Meanwhile, low- and medium-wage, insecure workers will not be able to carry on spending unless they can get their hands on unsecured credit, even if at less frenetic levels than had been occurring. Governments will want to see a return to credit boom as the most effective way of restoring consumer confidence while they continue to pursue policies making labour markets more flexible. They will be vulnerable to arguments from the financial sector that some relaxation of regulation will be needed if this is to happen. And, in a beggar-my-neighbour competition, individual governments will be tempted to ensure that they have slightly less onerous regulation than the others, in order to attract financial firms to base themselves within their jurisdictions in a competition that clearly leaves the firms in the more powerful position.

Furthermore, this will be a financial sector with a reduced number of major players, with very easy access to government. Some of the surviving firms will be those resulting from bank mergers encouraged and shaped by governments themselves during the course of the 2008 rescue packages. Governments that acquired banks in the bout of unforeseen nationalization that followed the October 2008 collapse do not intend to hold onto them under the old model of controlling the 'commanding heights' of the economy. The fact that big banks operate internationally will itself be a disincentive to that. It is, however, also unlikely that these banks will be privatized through general public share issues. They will most likely be levered into the hands of a small number of leading existing firms, either other banks or corporations in other sectors considered large enough to assume the huge burden of risk involved in contemporary financial capitalism.

Degrees of competition have varied very widely across the financial sector. In some parts there have been something approaching pure markets; in everyday, 'High Street' banking there has been more of a Chicago economy of domination by a small number of giant corporations. Many neoliberals argue that the problem has been too much regulation rather than too little. Regulation, they say, together with the tacit expectation that, in a democratic economy, governments could not allow major banks to fail, has enabled financial firms to take risks that they would have avoided if they had been totally on their own, required to take precautionary measures against each other's potential unreliability. While neoliberals tend to favour larger enterprises over smaller ones, they would never concede that some firms are 'too big to fail', as was repeatedly argued about the financial sector during the height of the crisis. They would have accepted the failures and bankruptcies as part of the way in which a market economy corrects itself and redistributes resources from the inefficient to the efficient.

In purely scientific terms, that argument is very strong. But it hardly addresses the reality that faces governments when an economy dominated by some very large firms in a sector like banking, which has implications across the economy and therefore represents certain public goods, goes into a major collapse. If it had been a true neoclassical market, with large numbers of players, self-correction by the market might have eased the situation without such extensive consequences. But we have a Chicago economy, not a neoclassical one. Caught between firms that have systemic importance in this way, but which remain responsible solely to their shareholders, and rejecting government action as a solution that is almost certain to make matters worse, strict neoliberals are left with little to say other than that the past two centuries should have produced a different, totally unregulated system of banking.

Far more realistic is what one might call the 'social democratic neoliberal' proposal that has emerged from some observers. This would essentially be a return to the US 1933 Glass-Steagall position, with a two-tier banking system: a group of presumably very large firms that are closely regulated to ensure that they do not take high risks, and that take care of the savings and investments of the great majority of individuals and small firms; and a separate sector of high-risk players, who are not permitted to have access to the savings of ordinary people, but who, with only the money of clients knowingly having their funds engaged in this way, can become very rich or go out of business depending on their performance in pure markets unprotected by government guarantees. It probably represents the best option for reconstructing the system in the immediate and medium term.

It is doubtful, however, whether it is viable in the long term. The problem is that bankers and politicians alike have eaten the fruit of the tree of knowledge of secondary markets. Bankers know, more than can have been envisaged in the 1980s, just how much wealth can be made trading in constantly expanded derivatives markets. Politicians know how valuable mass debt can be in insulating the purchasing power of relatively poor people from reductions in the welfare state and in labour regulation. How long can one expect the boundaries erected between safe mass banks and risky investment banks to last, when those boundaries are preventing bankers and politicians from reaping the benefits they came to understand in the 1990s and 2000s?

There will be erosion and slippage of any new boundaries. But governments now also know the damage that the secondary markets can do when they spiral out of control, as occurred in 2008–9. They will want some safeguards against a complete return to the deregulated model. There is therefore likely to be an incremental slip towards a more negotiated, voluntary regulatory system making use of the close relations that exist between governments and giant enterprises, to compensate for a gradual relaxation of regulation. To predict this is hardly crystal-ball-gazing: it is a general trend in government–firm relations right across the economy. Sharing neoliberal prejudices against government intervention, frightened at the impact of regulation on growth and believing in the superiority of private sector managers over themselves in nearly every respect, politicians increasingly rely on the conduct of giant firms for the achievement of many general social goals. True neoliberals do not like this kind of solution at all, as it interferes with the profit-maximization motive and encourages close relations between firms and governments that threaten the autonomy of the market economy. But important strands of business opinion favour it very much.

We have seen in this chapter how two forms of market failure contributed to the financial crisis: the meaning of price became distorted, and the speed of operations led to traders not being interested in acquiring information about what they were doing. But resolution of the crisis has introduced two further market failures. First, the need of efficient markets for low entry and exit barriers has been abused. Entry barriers are the more frequently discussed problem in relation to sectors dominated by giant firms; but *exit* barriers have played a particular role in this crisis. The extraordinary sums of money that were spent on rescuing banks were justified by the argument that the banks were 'too big to fail', in the sense that if they failed they would bring the whole economy down with them. This meant that barriers had to be erected against their exit. As many commentators noted, if banks have acquired this status, they are not compatible with the rules of the market economy.

Second, the bank rescue has involved yet another breach of the market principle that polity and economy, in particular governments and corporations, need to be kept separate from one another. And the longer-term solution to the financial problem is likely to require even more breaches of that principle. Corporations, responsible though they continue to be to their shareholders (or transitory share traders) alone, have emerged as key actors in maintaining the overall stability, not just of the economy, but of society in general.

6

From Corporate Political Entanglement to Corporate Social Responsibility

The problems presented by the political firm, the firm that has stepped out from being governed by the market to the point where it is a political actor in its own right, are not easily dealt with by any theoretical approaches in economic or political science. Within the latter, the main theory of political power, and not just in the formal process of elections, parties and governments, is that of political pluralism. It comes from the same intellectual stable as neoclassical economics, though it lacks the elegance of the economic argument, being based on a large number of empirical possibilities rather than the single theoretical one of the existence of pure markets. According to this theory, to prevent major inequalities of political power arising, it is important that power resources are scattered around a society in autonomous centres, and not aggregated into large blocs. Public decision-making then requires the assembly of numbers of these centres. Also as with economic theory, a more or less egalitarian economy is one of the conditions for political pluralism; a polity in which economic resources were very unequally shared would be likely to be one in which political power was also concentrated, economic resources being so easily capable of conversion into political ones.

During the late 1970s, the period when the Chicago approach was starting to assert itself in US antitrust law, two of the most prominent exponents of American political pluralism, Robert Dahl (1982) and Charles Lindblom (1977), warned that the large corporation was becoming a threat to the balance of democratic pluralism. Lindblom based his analysis not so much on the implications of the size of individual firms, as on the absolute dependence of governments for their popularity and legitimacy on economic success, and their belief that they depended for that success on the business community. Governments were therefore likely to listen intently and uncritically to whatever that community said it wanted from public policy.

Dahl and Lindblom were writing well before the rise of privatized Keynesianism and when the current trend towards economic globalization following the international deregulation of financial markets was just beginning. These processes have further enhanced the capacity of transnational corporations (TNCs) to translate their economic strength into political power. We have examined the role of privatized Keynesianism. We must now consider global firms. These acquire political power in two ways. First, they have some capacity to 'regime shop', that is to direct their investments to countries where they find the most favourable rules. Second, the global economy itself constitutes a space where governmental actors are (compared with the national level within stable nation-states) relatively weak and corporations therefore have more autonomy.

The first of the arguments here seems straightforward: if firms have a choice between two countries for maintaining their investments, they should be predicted to choose that which presents better opportunities for profit maximization, which will mean lower costs, and therefore lower levels of corporate taxation, of labour protection and social standards, and of environmental and other regulation. In the short run we should therefore expect a shift of investments from the more costly to the cheaper country. In the longer run the former should be expected to adjust its own standards downwards in order to be able to compete for investments with the cheaper country. The result would be a general lowering of standards to meet the preferences of multinational enterprises – a process often known as 'the race to the bottom'.

In reality, matters are nothing like as clear-cut as this. Existing investments in plant, distribution and supplier networks, as well as social links, are not so easily moved. Firms have what are called 'sunk costs' in their existing locations, and in order to move existing investments from one jurisdiction to another they need confidence that profits in the new location will be sufficient to outweigh these costs. The more likely threat is not a transfer of existing investments but a preference for the cheaper country for future new investments. Even here, there is not necessarily a consistent preference for the cheapest locations. Firms, especially those that are capable of strategy, choose in which market niches to locate themselves, and this does not always mean the lowest costs. The high quality of the goods or services being produced is often a criterion, and this may require highly paid staff with good working conditions, or a strong social infrastructure, requiring high taxation. It is therefore not the case that high-wage, high-tax economies have always lost out in competition for direct inward investment.

Nevertheless, this argument still places the initiative with the firms: it is their market strategy that determines (or at least strongly affects) whether particular government policies will be 'rewarded' with investment or not, whether these are policies for making available a population to work at low wages or one with high skills and secure lives. Globalization does not mean a race to the bottom, but it does increase the power of global firms in setting the rules of the race.

The second argument maintains that, there being no government at global level, TNCs are left fairly free to make what rules they like there, including deals they make between each other for setting standards or rules of trade. Since this is the level at which there is currently most economic dynamism, this regulation determined by global firms feeds back into national levels, undermining government authority.

This argument too is exaggerated. Alongside the growth of the global economy has come an increase in regulatory activity by international agencies whose members comprise national governments and which therefore constitute delegated governmental authority. Since the postwar period, some (but not much) of the work of the United Nations, and the activities of the World Bank and International Monetary Fund (IMF), have had some authority of this kind. The Organisation for Economic Co-Operation and Development (OECD), for long mainly a source of data and statistics on national economies, has gradually acquired more of an international policy-coordinating role – for example, in the field of corruption in governments' business deals with TNCs. Most recently, the World Trade Organization (WTO) has begun to regulate terms of international trade, though its authority extends more over governments than over corporations. Finally, at a level between the nation-state and the global level itself, there has been a growth of inter-governmental organizations regulating economic affairs in a more detailed way across world regions: the European Union (EU), the Association of South-East Asian Nations (ASEAN), the North American Free Trade Area (NAFTA), the organization of South American states called Mercosur – though of these only the EU has developed extensive policies across a wide range of fields. Global economic space is therefore not entirely without public regulation, but individual giant firms clearly occupy a more directly regulatory role at this level than at national levels.

When Robert Dahl considered the inability of pluralist theory to deal adequately with the political role of individual firms in the 1970s US economy, he looked for potential solutions in the organized capitalism of the Nordic economies. Here, firms exercised political influence mainly through business associations, partly at the sectoral level, but partly through peak associations representing the whole private sector. Because this representation was formal and open, it could be used to impose some kind of collective social responsibility on member firms in exchange for any success of their lobbying activities. In addition, lobbying through associations maintained a level playing field among firms, at least within a sector, and could not be used to secure anti-competitive privileges for individual companies with special links to politicians or public officials.

Dahl was here moving from US pluralist theory to the northern European approach of neo-corporatism. While most often used for the analysis of relations between trade unions and organized employers, the concept of interest representation through organizations that simultaneously lobbied and imposed codes of behaviour on members could also be used more generally to describe the politics of business in certain contexts. While neo-corporatism might avoid some of the political problems presented by single-firm political action, it presents a new one: that whole sectors might become privileged at the expense of others, or functional economic interests privileged over other kinds of interest (for example, the environment). As Mancur Olson argued in his book *The Rise and Decline of Nations* (1982), in a market economy organizations of particular interests operate by means of rent-seeking behaviour: that is, extracting gains for their members from the general public without offering anything in return. In other words, to use the term that we developed in Chapter 2, they produce a negative externality, which they would not be permitted to do by the pure market. They would abstain from this only if their membership was so extensive within the society concerned ('encompassing' in Olson's term) that they would have to reinternalize any negative consequences of their action. This means a situation in which there is not enough of the society outside the group's membership onto which negative consequences can be dumped. This would be the case where neo-corporatist structures operated most successfully.

Olson's concept of 'encompassing' organizations assumes a manageable and definable universe, linking fiscal and

monetary policy and the scope of firms, across which organizations can be said to be encompassing. Throughout most
of the history of industrial societies the nation-state provided
such a universe, but no longer. Neo-corporatism is severely
challenged by the global economy and, in particular, the
global firm. Neo-corporatist organizations can respond positively to this kind of situation by shifting their point of
activity to a higher level, such as the EU, joining forces with
their opposite numbers in other nation-states to recapture
encompassingness. But incentives to do this have been weak.
Governments, trade unions and smaller firms remain organized primarily at national levels, and governments and
unions have to respond to national constituencies. In any
case, even the EU falls far short of being global. It is difficult
for any system of organized interests that is not itself global
to achieve encompassingness.

A further problem with neo-corporatism is that, being
based on associations representing existing industries and
sectors, it loses effectiveness at times of rapid economic
and technical change. The old, organized sectors of the
economy become less important – or, worse, their organizations try to slow down a decline that will be inevitable.
Meanwhile, new sectors are not yet organized, and may
not even see themselves as sectors. For example, what we
now see as the biotechnical industry was growing up for
several years before its existence as such was noted. Now it
and other new industries, such as information technology,
have acquired self-awareness and developed organizations.
But it remains the case that, at any moment during a period
of high change and innovation, old, declining sectors will be
better represented by sector-level organizations than new,
dynamic ones.

As with the case of standards discussed in Chapter 3,
individual TNCs, rather than associations, have become the
main carriers of business interests. At an initial view, globalization and deregulation are about the triumph of the market,
at the expense of both corporatism and the state; but, once
again, at a second look we see that it is the individual giant

firm, rather than the pure market that has emerged as dominant. This fundamentally important development for both economy and polity distorts the level playing field among firms – that vital condition for a true market without major impediments to entry – considerably limiting the chances of influence for small ones, which need business associations in order to get anywhere near political elites. Individual TNCs, in contrast, are given a strong incentive and possibility to act politically. Paradoxically, while the free market and political pluralism seem to belong to the same family, in practice neo-corporatist associational representation is better able to maintain a level playing field among firms and therefore restrain market distortions than is a pluralist system operating under Chicago conditions with few restraints on firm size.

From the perspective of pluralist political theory, firms constitute 'lobbies', and the kind of role that giant firms are able to play in the global economy makes them disturbingly powerful ones, threatening the balance of both democracy and pluralism. This was the burden of the critique of Dahl and Lindblom, and of a large number of subsequent critics – including the earlier chapters of this book. But the role of today's global giants cannot be subsumed under the concept of lobbying. The origins of the term 'lobby' lie in the literal meaning of the word, denoting a room or hallway outside the room where the real action is taking place. The original reference is to the space outside a ruler's council chamber or court, where persons wishing to plead a cause with members of the council would seek a chance to speak with them on their way in. Those pleading would have no right of admission to the chamber itself. The representatives of today's TNCs are not in the lobby, outside the real decision-making space of government, at all. They are right inside the room of political decision-making. They set standards, establish private regulatory systems, act as consultants to government, even have staff seconded to ministers' offices. In Chapter 4 we saw how, in response to the criticism that governments have become out of touch with business practices, earlier rules to ensure a separation between government officials and business interests have been 'modernized'.

An example of how firms have been allowed to become insiders to politics concerns the financing of election campaigns by corporate donors in the USA. Elections in that country are extremely expensive, as virtually unrestrained use is made of costly television programmes and other high-tech communications. Further, party structures in the USA being weak, individual candidates are left on their own to raise their campaign funds far more than in European democracies. The existence of primary campaigns, in which candidates compete to win the votes of their party's registered voters for the right to stand as the party's candidate, intensify this further, because the party itself cannot fund such campaigns. Politicians seeking re-election are desperate for money. Firms with business interests that will be affected by government decisions and legislation offer donations to causes, which are then channelled into the campaign funds of politicians who have followed the firms' 'advice'. For genuine neoliberals this should be as grave an offence to the free market as state extra-legal intervention in a firm's affairs. That it is not generally seen by US citizens in this way but just as 'business as usual', perfectly compatible with claims that the USA constitutes the world's paragon of democratic practice, is a testament to the victory of corporate politics even over thought processes.

The lobbying concept is inadequate for further reasons. First, it is usually assumed that those engaged in lobbying are members of the polity of the nation-state concerned, or physically within it and therefore subject to its authority for the time being. This is not the case with TNCs bargaining over the terms of their investments. International law requires firms to have a place somewhere on the planet where they have their formal location, but from that base they can deal with governments across the world, never putting themselves into a position of subordination to their authority, unless and until they set up facilities. During the crucial period of negotiations, when they are deciding among a number of potential locations for an investment, they remain external and therefore do not 'lobby' for terms, an action implying at least formal subordination. Their relations are more like those of ambassadors of other states, but they cannot be assimilated to this concept as it belongs only to the world of political entities.

Second, it is difficult to apply the concept of a lobby to the relationship between large global firms and a global polity seen as constituted by nation-states and organizations formed by treaties among them. This can perhaps be seen most clearly in the autonomous role played by individual corporations in setting standards, which is a kind of legislative activity. These corporations exist out there *alongside* the international and transnational agencies, not generally subordinate to them.

Third, when large corporations from the advanced countries invest in very poor countries, there is usually a major imbalance between the institutions of the corporations and those of the local state. The former will be well equipped and staffed, with a high level of resources, and with clear hierarchies and internal procedures. The local state is likely to have very low levels of resources and poor means of internal communications and enforcement. In such circumstances it is very difficult for that state to live up to the legal fiction that it constitutes an 'authority' and the investing firm a private entity subject to that authority. The firm is likely to be able to pick and choose which local laws it obeys and which it ignores, as enforcement and inspection are likely to be poor. The firm becomes its own law-enforcement agency. This imbalance can also work the other way. Within the society governed by the local state there may well be only meagre political debate, while the home base of the investing firm may be involved in lively controversy, even over affairs in the country where the firm is investing. For example, a Scandinavian firm employing child labour in an African country is almost certain to experience more difficulties about the issue at home than it is in the country where the abuse is occurring. In response to such domestic pressure the firm might well become a more vigorous guardian of children's rights than the African government. Again, the firm becomes its own law-enforcement agency – and has become hopelessly implicated in politics, even if it does not want to be.

Fourth, this last example raises the general issue of corporate social responsibility (CSR). This was discussed briefly in the previous chapter in connection with debates over shareholder responsibility, but we now need to examine it in more detail.

Corporate Social Responsibility as a Political Theory of the Firm?

The idea of corporate social responsibility was, for a long time, developed by firms themselves as something that they did to fulfil certain obligations to society. As such, observers have been suspicious of it as an emanation from corporate PR departments trying to attract attention away from dubious behaviour. It often is little more than this, but it also contains elements that deserve to be taken more seriously – both as a problematic manifestation of corporate power and, paradoxically, as a useful instrument in the hands of critics of corporate behaviour faced with political systems highly vulnerable to corporate lobbying.

CSR has to be distinguished from charitable activities, or the establishment of charitable trusts and foundations by firms. These activities are usually governed by separate bodies of law, recognizing and regulating the existence of a particular form of publicly oriented activity that is part of neither the state nor profit-making. CSR is undertaken by firms within the ambit of normal company law, directors and senior management using their capacity for strategy to pursue public policy goals. In seeking concepts by which this process might be understood, some authors have developed the idea of 'corporate citizenship'. This can have a banal meaning, signifying little more than that firms ought to behave like good citizens. But Crane et al., in their 2008 book *Corporations and Citizenship*, took the term to a higher pitch of analysis. Strictly speaking, firms cannot 'be' citizens, as in democracies this quality belongs solely to the individual human beings who possess the right to vote. But Crane et al. see firms as administering the general rights of citizens, in so far as firms enter the field of making corporate-level public policy, which is what CSR amounts to. The idea remains deeply problematic, as citizens have no formal capacity to access the corporation (which remains governed by corporate law, recognizing only the rights of shareholders) in the way that they can in theory put political pressure on governments. On the other hand, firms can be responsive to citizens qua customers.

'Corporate citizenship' also suggests firms having both the rights and the powers of citizens, and sees them as definitely part of the polity and not confined to the market. This is useful for a realistic approach to contemporary corporate behaviour. When they are making their own regulation through standards, or acting not just as lobbies but as insiders to the public decision-making process, firms can be seen as exercising a kind of citizenship right. When their critics argue that, if these are the rights they are claiming, then they must expect to be subjected to demands of good behaviour going beyond their need to maximize profits within the market, they are making the reasonable point that citizenship rights need to be accompanied by responsibilities.

Some see this kind of discussion as alarming. Is democratic citizenship not limited to human individuals? How can corporations, even if they are regarded as individuals in law, be compared to human citizens? Is it implied that they should have the vote? The most obvious means available to societies for dealing with externalities is to have government and law responsible for them – whether through regulation, taxation or other means. The state is charged with responsibility for the public realm, in particular those goods that are held in common as collective goods by a defined community. Therefore, should firms define a CSR role for themselves, or should they concentrate on profit maximization, leaving it to government to pursue public goals – both the creation of positive externalities and the suppression of negative ones? This is closely related to a further question: should a firm be required to maximize shareholder value alone, or should its mandate be extended to embrace wider criteria of value?

One position in this debate was prominently articulated by the leading Chicago neoliberal Milton Friedman, who argued (1970), not just that firms had no *duties* beyond shareholder value maximization, but that they had no *right* to go beyond that and decide wider social goals. There are two parts to this. The first maintains that if firms pursue goals other than strict profit maximization, they will become inefficient. The implications of this for CSR will be considered later. First, we are concerned with the second part, the relationship between CSR and the polity: that firms have no right to second-guess government's responsibility to determine the extra-economic criteria that should govern their behaviour. On this part of his argument Friedman would have found ready allies among state-centred socialists. It raises two problems: does government have the capacity to enforce its regulation on global firms? And what are the implications of Friedman's argument for firms' rights to engage in political action?

Friedman's view that firms should not interfere with public policy questions was naive in a world where they engage in massive lobbying activities precisely to ensure certain public policy directions. He would, however, probably have argued that this was in order provided the lobbying was directed at aiding shareholder value maximization: if a firm can secure a regulatory environment that suits what it wants to do, it will be better able to maximize its profits. But, in intervening in politics and society in this way, the firm is certainly stepping outside the frame of straightforward market exchanges. As a result of its actions, the views of legislators and officials are changed, or the ability of a particular party to succeed electorally is affected, or large numbers of people have switched their opinions over an issue. Advocates of CSR can therefore be seen as seeking a route to something beyond profit maximization in a world where giant corporations are acquiring a political and social capacity beyond the reach of governments, and where governments have learned neoliberal lessons warning them against intervening in the economy. In such a world, it seems, only the major corporation is in a position effectively to carry the torch for values.

This discussion directs our attention to something very important: not everything in a polity that has democratic elections is necessarily democratic. It is common in democratic societies for leaders to develop tortuous arguments to claim that everything they do is democratic, so wounding is the charge of acting undemocratically. Because they emerged from an electoral process able to command a majority in a parliament, political leaders claim that they have a democratic mandate for everything that they do, that their hand in affairs guarantees that these are suffused with democratic quality, even if these were things very different from what they claimed they would do at the previous election. This democratic legitimation is then used to discredit critics, even if these actually represent a majority of opinion. This procedure is seen as necessary to maintain the concept of democracy, but it would be more honest and involve less distortion to language if we acknowledged that there was a democratic and a non-democratic part to politics in democracies. This would also enable us to confront honestly the fact that the political power of corporations constitutes a widely accepted but highly undemocratic feature of our de facto constitutions. The role of large, powerful firms could then be analysed more openly, and it could be admitted that there is a realm of non-democratic citizenship in which they are prominent actors but from which the great majority of individual human citizens is excluded.

The fact, already discussed above, that nation-states no longer constitute the whole of the public domain, is also relevant here. John Ruggie – a political scientist appointed in 2005 to be the Representative of the United Nations Secretary-General on Business and Human Rights – has argued (2007; 2009) that the very system of states is becoming embedded in a broader and deepening international arena concerned with the production of global goods, in which corporations are major players alongside states. Global firms have become so powerful that they cannot avoid political attention, even if political actors can exercise little direct leverage on them. In such a context governments and international agencies seek the support of firms to do their work. A major example of this is the Global Compact that the UN reached with a large number of global corporations, and which tries to tie firms down to a specified set of CSR obligations. The mechanism is weak, as a study of it by Rasche and Kell shows (2010), because it lacks enforcement capacity, but Ruggie argues that this kind of engagement with corporations marks a step forward towards greater public governance rather than a submission to corporate power.

These ideas belong essentially to political theory, but they will be approached here from the perspective of the mainly economic ideas that have dominated this book. I shall start from the idea that CSR is best seen as behaviour by firms that voluntarily takes account of the externalities produced by their market behaviour, externalities being defined as in Chapter 2 to refer to results of market transactions that are not themselves embodied in such transactions. CSR is therefore essentially 'corporate externality recognition'. This gets us beyond slogans and PR exercises and enables us to understand what CSR is claiming to achieve. For a firm to reduce production of a negative externality – or to increase production of a positive one – by definition requires it to take action that is outside its immediate market relationships, and that will cost it something, for which it will not immediately reap rewards. How can a profit-maximizing firm be expected to take action of such a kind? Or, more positively, what kinds of pressure can be brought to bear to make firms take such actions, given that by themselves they are unlikely to do so in other than a cosmetic way?

The fundamental point is that no firms, even giant TNCs, act with complete autonomy. However powerful they are, they need to sell their products if they are to maximize shareholder value, and this can make them both vulnerable and sensitive to certain pressures. Can we assume a demand for socially responsible behaviour from somewhere in firms' markets? Do we, in particular, have any reason to assume that customers might care about the moral behaviour of the firms from which they buy goods and services? Might there be such a thing as a consumer taste for moral corporate behaviour? Since tastes are shaped partly by fashion, can we imagine a fashion for CSR?

There is considerable research evidence that there is indeed a consumer preference for what we might call 'CSR goods'. The number of High Street companies boasting of their environmental friendliness and also the popularity of Fairtrade brands are both major examples. It can become 'non-cool' to buy products from, or invest in or work for firms that have acquired a reputation for bad behaviour – for producing negative externalities, in our jargon. The possibilities of this situation have been perceived by several cause groups. Fashion can be swayed by many factors, and avoiding brands that are associated with bad labour or environmental practices can be at least as important a determinant of fashion decisions as avoiding last year's colours. 'Green' can be the new black. This might appear to trivialize some important causes, and fashion is by definition temporary: what happens if it suddenly becomes chic to wear clothes known to be produced by child slave labour? This is a risky, unreliable path. However, given that many people would sooner do good in the world than harm, campaigns centred on environmental and third world labour issues have started to challenge bad corporate behaviour by activating their customers. It is often lamented that we are today so obsessed with individualistic consumerism that we do not care about wider issues. But the two can be combined, and we can express values and make political statements that have real consequences through our consumption choices. To paraphrase Naomi Hertz (2001): 'We might not vote anymore, but we all go shopping!'

Similar arguments can apply to investors and employees. Investors do not necessarily have to have an ethical taste themselves; they only have to believe that it exists, or will soon exist, among consumers, and they will start to prefer investing in companies with CSR reputations. We might almost talk of a secondary market in ethical corporate behaviour. Any response by investors of this kind refers to a further and highly relevant aspect of the giant but dynamic corporation. Such firms do not just supply goods and services in response to existing demand; they try to shape that demand – that is what 'marketing' means. Firms therefore have choices, not only over to which taste niches they wish to *respond*, but over the kinds of niches that they wish to try to *create*. The firm does this actively as an organization.

It is very common for CSR studies to distinguish between short-term profit maximization likely to be pursued by shareholder interests (particularly those embodied in stock markets) and a longer-term interest that these are in danger of neglecting. They may be cared for by institutional share-holders, venture capitalists or senior management, but the spot market as such cannot easily cope with the long term. Normally, long-term actions require a capacity of the firm qua organization temporarily (but only temporarily) to sec-ond-guess the market, or rather to combine market and organizational action. The firm receives messages from certain points in its environment that it will need to incur certain short-term costs in order to respond to an externality if it is to pursue its own long-term interests. The interesting issue is then: from what points? By being alert to social issues that are not only current but might be developing in future, or to social groups that are weak today but might acquire power tomorrow, firms may be able to anticipate change. Engagement in CSR activities can be used to demonstrate to investors that the firm has its ear to the ground and is engag-ing with potential customers – in general, and not only with reference to ethical issues.

These arguments seem to resolve the other part of the Friedman problem – that pursuit of CSR risks inefficiency – and also the basic CSR dilemma. However, they beg the question of how, from among the mass of possibilities, firms are to select those that give a sure guide to future market opportunities. In the last analysis, interpretation of a corporation's response to a social issue would be in the hands of individual executives and their personal judgements. In the previous chapter we examined the arguments of Michael Jensen concerning the moral hazards involved here. He saw CSR as precisely the kind of issue on which managers will seize in order to acquire autonomy to pursue their private ends at the expense of the shareholders. But this argument depends on the assumption that the signals conveyed in share prices are always superior to managerial assessments of a firm's prospects, because the former is a neutral market mechanism, while the human judgement of managers and other professionals will be swayed by personal concerns. But in practice this will not always be the case; in conditions of uncertainty, share prices may sometimes reflect mutually reinforced erroneous perceptions, while managers may have sound professional knowledge. An example would be the final stages of the dot.com bubble, when ignorance was driving share prices. Even more powerfully, the recent financial crisis has entitled us to doubt the quality of the knowledge governing spot markets; this provides continuing scope for managers to seek some autonomy from them and to act entrepreneurially.

CSR may also help firms develop consumer trust. It is difficult for customers, small investors and others to determine whether or not firms are honest, but firms can take a number of steps to acquire a reputation for probity, and adopting prominent CSR strategies can be a means of doing this. Customers may believe that a firm that engages in good works in the community has a kind of corporate conscience, and would not engage in dishonest practices. Investors may do the same. In other words, firms may find it rational to accept the short-term costs of reducing negative (or increasing positive) externalities flowing from their activities in order to realize long-term trust gains. Of course, what firms need is a *reputation* for good behaviour rather than good behaviour itself. This can mean using claims and self-advertisement without actually changing behaviour. Since the actual pursuit of CSR also requires expenditure on its advertisement if it is to be known by customers, investors and others, it will always be cheaper to pursue reputation alone. This further trust problem has led to the growth of a specialized set of institutional trust mechanisms for monitoring CSR practices, with various firms and voluntary bodies developing benchmarks and scorecards.

   This pressure on firms sometimes to treat CSR as something more than a PR exercise has not resulted from the uncoordinated responses of millions of consumers. As John Campbell has argued in 'Why Would Corporations Behave in Socially Responsible Ways?' (2007), pressure comes from several elements in a firm's social and political context. At one level, it has had to be organized. Groups campaigning around environmental issues, fair trade with developing countries and labour conditions in supply chains have worked hard to mobilize customers, drawing attention to unethical and environmentally damaging, and occasionally to good, behaviour. This marks a shift from corporate social responsibility in an agenda framed by firms themselves to corporate social accountability framed by groups of citizens. It creates a genuinely new political arena (Néron 2010; Vogel 2008). As the corporation becomes a political actor, so it becomes a centre of political action in its own right. Critics of corporate behaviour target firms directly, as well as indirectly via parties and governments – though the existence of laws and regulations often provides a vital springboard for campaigning action. As the corporation operates in both markets and politics, so its critics operate through market pressure as well as through direct political action.

   It is even possible that – only sometimes and in only some cases – firms may be more responsive than governments to pressures of this kind. There are two reasons for this. First, governments may become so obsessed with ensuring they provide no impediments to enterprise that they establish a general strategy of leaving firms alone as much as possible. Meanwhile, some firms are becoming sensitive to the market opportunities offered by subtle nuances of taste changes among consumers. There was an interesting example of this during the controversy over genetically modified foods in several European countries. Some governments were still defending the use of GMO while supermarket chains, responding to widespread consumer concerns, were declaring their shelves to be free of GMO products.

A further advantage of campaigns directed at giant corporations rather than governments is that these usually have an important built-in international component, as the firms themselves are transnational. Consumers and campaigners can organize internationally, and the objects of concern are often in a number of developing countries. These campaigns therefore constitute the early germination of the seeds of a transnational civil society. Meanwhile, governments, parties and political systems remain doggedly national; they are defined by the nation-state and are dedicated to pursuing the interests of that nation-state, any solidary action being of very marginal importance and existing mainly at very formal diplomatic levels, remote from civil society.

Finally, it was noted above that the role of corporations in politics is part of the non-democratic component of the constitution. So too is the oppositional politics around the corporation. The vitality of campaigns and cause groups is evidence of a lively, pluralistic civil society, but it is not democracy in the formal sense of electoral processes within which all adults have a right to participate. Most of this book has been about the triangle of state, market and corporation. In the course of this chapter we have seen the appearance of a fourth point, leading to a potential quadrilateral of forces: civil society. Where does this fit, and how does it relate to the field of states and politics?

7

Values and Civil Society

In previous chapters we have concentrated on the problems of a market- and corporation-led society. The normal conclusion of such arguments in left-of-centre thinking is to demonstrate the need for action by the democratic state. But what if we are uncertain as to the integrity and capacity of political institutions? There are today two broad sets of reasons why we should be uncertain. The first, associated with the political right and the Virginia school of public choice theory, concentrates on the likelihood that politicians and other public officials will pursue their own career goals rather than any social good, and on the difficulty anyway of achieving social good through the top-down processes typical of government action. This logic then arrives at the market as a superior device for tackling problems. The second set, associated with the political left, shares much of the thinking of the right concerning the fallibility of politics and politicians, but places particular emphasis on the role of entanglements between politics and business in the corruption of democracy. But, thinkers on the left maintain their historic reservations concerning the capacity of markets to solve problems – unless heavily corrected by regulation, which in turn becomes vulnerable again to the weakness of too much contact between business and politics.

The previous chapters of this book have demonstrated that this familiar opposition of market and state is becoming threadbare, for two main reasons. First, where the neoliberal political right points to 'markets' it is often really indicating corporations. Second, the state, seen for so long by the left as the source of countervailing power against markets and corporations, is today likely to be the committed ally of giant corporations, whatever the ideological origins of the parties governing the state.

It is claimed for both political democracy and the market that they can harness the individual strivings of powerful and talented individuals to a collective good. Democracy does this by requiring aspirant rulers to seek popular legitimation through periodic elections and, between times, to accept continuing investigation, scrutiny and criticism. The market achieves it by requiring the owners of property to maintain their wealth by producing goods and services that customers freely want to buy. This is not the way in which the roles of democracy and markets are usually described. Both are usually represented as means by which the mass of the people achieve certain goals. This is a very consumerist view. Both political power and economic wealth existed long before attempts were made to subject them to democracy and the market; and neither of these latter can be said to have predominated in human history, which has mainly been the story of the domination and exploitation of the many by the powerful few. Dealing with that phenomenon comes before individual citizens 'getting something' out of either public policy or the market. It is also common in political and economic discussion to set the market alongside the private individual, and the state with the collective public. On deeper reflection, both can be seen to be concerned with something public – dealing with power – and both can be appropriated by the private.

The conflict between the individual and the collective is frequently depicted in ethical terms, though it is an argument that can be seen in contrasting ways. In many systems of thought (for example, most traditional religion, historical conservatism, socialism) the collective embodies moral values that prevent individual selfishness from disrupting order and hurting others. In others (dissenting religions, classic liberalism, opponents of totalitarian regimes of all kinds) the individual human embodies values of personal authenticity against a cynical collectivity.

Both images can be true. But the moral individual fighting an amoral collectivity is doing so on behalf of an imagined moral community. The idea of an ethic of total individualism in the sense of selfishness is a contradiction in terms, or at least a limiting case. The necessarily collective nature of human life imposes on us a need for constraints on our conduct. The human infant is unable to survive at all without the care of other humans, but even in adulthood individuals whose lives do not involve some degree of interdependence with others quickly die. But within these interdependent groups there is a constant temptation to seek personal advantage by taking from or acting violently against others. We need each other's good behaviour, and although state and market help us in this by providing police forces and economic incentives, these are neither always effective nor present at every moment. And we need to demonstrate that we behave well ourselves to avoid suspicion that we might be seeking to cheat. Criminals and confidence tricksters thrive on exploiting these systems of mutual demonstrations of good behaviour, but for most of the time we get by with them. Their cumulative effect is to impart an expectation of morality in the institutions of collective life, or at least in the way that collective institutions are publicly discussed. In private it may be very different, and we may consider using the most unscrupulous means, if we think we could get away with them. The error of Niccolò Machiavelli was to write for public consumption the cynical advice on how to conduct government that should normally be whispered into a ruler's ear. History has rewarded him by regarding him as both the symbol of political ruthlessness and the founder of the rational analysis of political action – not that there is any necessary contradiction in that.

In this view, it is the conditions of collective life that impose ethical behaviour on individuals, the individuals themselves simultaneously trying to escape these restraints in order to steal a march on each other, being grateful that the restraints on others exist, and being eager to demonstrate that they accept the restraints in order to be seen as 'good'.

But collectivities can also be used by individuals to seek selfish ends, by turning the power of a particular collectivity against others, from whose expropriation they might gain. A collectivity can be used for aggressive purposes against outsiders, or against internal minorities, or against unpopular individuals. The language of high moral purpose can be used to justify such actions. There is no inherent moral superiority of collective over individual, or vice versa, but it is the existence of collectivities that provides the forum in which debate over the ethical quality of life can take place.

Politics and markets provide contrasting approaches to these dilemmas. We expect actors in the political arena to talk in ethical terms and to provide value-based rationales for their actions and goals. We are shocked and ill at ease if they use nakedly cynical language. In democracies the nature of the relationship between power-holders, power-contenders and the general public imposes these norms; but even autocracies and dictatorships often like to present their actions in this way. It need not be true, but, at least in democracies, it makes possible and even privileges discussion in ethical terms. The collectivities to which political action is oriented – most importantly nation-states – are usually defined by political actors in moral terms and endowed with moral qualities, particularly in terms of members of the society accepting responsibilities for each other, primarily through welfare states. But these collectivities can behave in unethical ways towards other collectivities or towards minorities within the nation-state itself.

The market, in contrast, is amoral. Any goals or forms of behaviour are acceptable to it, provided they can be financed. The only child pornographer who is unacceptable to the market is one who has no money. On the other hand, the collectivity of the market is potentially universal. It practises no exclusion on grounds of nationality, ethnicity, gender, age, disability or anything else other than ability to pay. And, if the market is more or less perfect, it requires all its participants to abide by common rules that prevent any one actor from harming others. The relation of markets and states to values is therefore complex. But values are important, as we shall see, to the search for ways out of the box presented to us by the aligned forces of states, markets and firms. We must therefore enquire more closely into their place in society.

For most of human history religion has provided the central framework within which people address such issues. It has done so by subordinating concerns about relations among humans to the greater one of responsibility before God. The task of religious organizations is then to interpret the will of God and its implications for responsibilities to other humans. This provides a powerful frame, which can also be used to justify inhumane actions. Religious values are usually oriented to collectivities of some kind, towards which moral obligations are owed. But, as with states, these collectivities can be defined narrowly, permitting or even requiring exclusion of or opposition to outsiders. Religions also differ in how much latitude they allow their followers in working out their own answers to value questions. If they allow much, the guiding power of the religion is diluted. If they allow very little, they have a problem of enforcement. If they are to stay strictly within the world of values, this power derives solely from the fear of God and what He might do to the disobedient human soul. If this proves inadequate, religions fall back on other forms of power, including the power of ostracism from community.

Dominant religions have often relied on, or co-opted, the state as an enforcement arm. Within the western world this dependence of the church on state power culminated eventually in the at least partial loss of monopoly over the definition of values. Gradually – or sometimes as with the French Revolution abruptly – the state, which had previously presented itself as the protector of its favoured church, now itself directly assumed the sole role as the promulgator and champion of values. As part of this the state ceased to be legitimated as the private property of a monarch, and started to be presented and legitimated as the possession of all, a *res publica*, a 'public thing', ultimately as a democracy. The state was proposed as the perfect embodiment of collective space.

In large part this remains our situation. A public debate about what 'ought' to be done in some moral sense is usually a debate about what government ought to do, or what it should encourage people to do, or at least make space for them to do. In democracies this emerges through debate and conflict; but, as noted above, in dictatorships governments themselves choose with surprising frequency to clothe their actions and declarations in ethical terms. Completely overt cynicism is unusual.

The historical role of philosophical advocates of the free market in this debate has *not* been to declare that moral outcomes are irrelevant to an individual's right to secure his or her private goals. Rather, it is to argue that, provided markets are near-perfect, the outcome of a mass of individuals' selfish behaviour will be consistent with overall public welfare.

Following my practice throughout this book, I do not accept that 'the firm' is just a subheading within a discussion of 'the market'. The place of the firm in questions of value is quite distinct from that of the market. It can be regarded as an actor that stands outside the realm of value, just pursuing its profits, and relying on the market to ensure that the sum of a mass of profit-making activities is a good collective outcome. But, as we saw in the previous chapter, corporate social responsibility – if it is anything more than a PR exercise, which it often is not – offers firms a different and ambiguous relationship with values. On the one hand, CSR suggests ethical obligations being placed on firms; on the other, it gives them the power to decide aspects of the moral agenda. For example, a supermarket chain might decide to devote considerable attention to the 'dolphin-friendly' nature of the fishing methods used to catch its tuna, but silently press price reductions on third world suppliers of clothing that imply starvation wages for their employees.

The aristocracy of pre-revolutionary France developed the concept of *noblesse oblige*, according to which, in exchange for its privileged social position, the nobility would accept a series of moral obligations in its behaviour towards the rest of society. But this was an entirely voluntary matter; nobility decided the content of these obligations; and no external force could impose them on it. CSR plays a rather similar role today, especially but not only in developing countries. Firms decide that they will select a number of values to which they will commit themselves; if they change their minds and do not want to continue in this course, they just stop; and they appraise their own success. But the existence and then critical discussion of CSR establishes the relevance of moral criteria within business behaviour, and opens the possibility of ethical debate in a manner excluded from the idea of *noblesse oblige*.

This, then, is the complex structure that the twentieth century has bequeathed us for the public discussion of issues of value. First, at some points and in some places, strong, formal religious organizations still stand for an eternal and infinite – though frequently intolerant and bigoted – sense of values in the public realm. Today, this is particularly the case in the USA, parts of Africa and in the Islamic world; far less so in Europe, Russia, Latin America, China and Japan; India stands somewhere in between. But in all liberal democracies religion has been required not to challenge the right of the democratic state to interpret the values that will predominate. Oddly, the modern state where that secular priority is today forcefully challenged is the one whose constitution insists most strongly on the separation of the state from church: the USA.

Second, the political arena retains its position as the forum in which most people in secularized societies expect to work through publicly relevant moral issues, with the state bearing responsibility to deal with moral problems. But states in liberal democracies do not demand an authoritarian control over the articulation of values; they too, like some religions, leave space. Third, the market is in large part morally neutral or amoral, but it does discipline behaviour away from selfishness of outcome if not of purpose, and, in its blind way, is hostile to discrimination and exclusion. Finally, many corporations engage in CSR, which, in a small way but increasingly, offers a new public space for value conflict and contestation alongside the formal political arena. The realm of values is therefore a fragmented and contested one, with few groups in a position to impose orthodoxy. This provides the opening for a large range of interests beyond those favoured by state, market or firm to gain access.

In modern democracies, especially multicultural ones, there is an uncontrollable jumble of claims on behalf of various rival, or simply different, values. Some would say that there is a 'market' in values, but since there is nothing analogous to prices to link the demand for and supply of values, the uses of the idea of market here are very limited. But if there were to be such a market, would we prefer it to be one of perfect competition among many suppliers of values, or a 'Chicago' market, with three or four monopoly suppliers? We have tendencies towards both in many contemporary societies. On the one hand is the inchoate mass of campaigning groups, existing usually on slender resources, challenging dominant orthodoxy and engaging in conflicts over values like little enterprises trying to find market niches. On the other hand, public debate in many of our societies is dominated by a small number of corporate media enterprises, with other giant firms limiting the scope of serious debate among political parties in the manner described elsewhere in this book. It is in the former, in the richness of fragmentation that our main hopes to challenge the dominance of politicized corporate power lies. A further way of securing some protection against domination is to ensure that no one realm can dominate all the others, and that those commanding one realm cannot easily extend their control over another. At the present time this means challenging the claim of states to be the primary definers of value, and of firms to be permitted privileged access to the state and to be the organizations to which public tasks should be entrusted.

Civil Society

This brings us to an important concept: civil society, which, in its early twenty-first-century sense, deals with this question of both diversity and balance. The Aristotelian idea of the *polis* that lies at its heart signified all areas of public life, but using 'public' in the sense of a restricted, identified public, not a universal one. This was the ordered life of the city-state, where free male citizens dealt together with collective tasks. It included all three institutions discussed above that enabled people to transcend the private. This public was contrasted with the private, in the sense of the individual and the immediate family or household. Polity, values (religion) and market are all found within the *polis*, held in a certain balance.

When Aristotle was translated into Latin, which took place in the city-state of sixteenth-century Florence, the translator translated *polis* as *societas civilis*: 'civil society'. In following centuries the city-states of Europe became overwhelmed – as had the Greek ones during Rome's imperial period – by states that stood outside and over the rest of society. Aristocratic and monarchic elites monopolized control of the state within their family groupings, and weakened the towns which had preserved something of the public unity of market, polity and values. The state became at best detached from the rest of the public sphere, at worst a part of the household of the ruler. Therefore, when the concept civil society began to be used again, in the nineteenth century, it usually excluded the state: the concept had been stood on its head. For Karl Marx civil society *became* the market: relationships of exchange that alienate man from his species life. Oddly, however, Aristotle's own Greek word, *polis*, continued to provide the words polity, politics, policy, police.

The concept returned again to prominence in the late twentieth century, among thinkers (initially in central Europe and Latin America) trying to identify a realm of dialogue and human exchange *excluded by polity and market alike*, the latter being seen as both alienated exchange and large corporations. So Marx's account itself had now been stood on its head. Today, not only in social philosophy but in common parlance, 'civil society' usually denotes those organizations and informal groupings that concern themselves with public affairs, but which operate outside the power of both state and firm. Significantly, they have become known by the nonsensical name 'non-governmental organizations' (NGOs). Better is the German term *Bürgerinitiativen*, 'citizens' initiatives'. Whether civil society now includes religious organizations is left ambiguous – they are usually included when they have lost their power, which reinforces the idea of civil society as 'the power of the powerless'. This phrase itself was coined in the 1980s by the Czech writer, civil activist and sometime president of his country, Václav Havel, to refer to the civil society outside the party-state that then existed in central and eastern Europe. Civil society includes, though extends further than, the voluntary sector. It defines all those extensions of the scope of human action beyond the private that lack recourse to the primary contemporary means of exercising power: the state and the firm.

This approach to civil society was captured and developed in a project organized by Jürgen Kocka at the Wissenschaftszentrum Berlin in the early years of this century, and well synthesized in his 2004 article 'Civil society in historical perspective'. Pointing out that at different historical periods the term has had different meanings, he stresses that today it identifies a sphere connected to but separate from economy, state and private life. It is oriented towards public conflict, discourse, compromise and understanding, recognizing plurality, difference and tension as legitimate, operating nonviolently. This is the space in which a value-oriented critique of market, state and corporation can be conducted in contemporary democracies. States and firms do dominate our societies, but there is a lively field of contention. Challenges to domination can be made, concepts of public goals explored and turned into practical projects, against the state's claim to monopoly of the legitimate interpretation of collective values, and against the firm's claim that the conversion of values into the maximization of shareholders' interests is as good as life can get.

Battle can be joined in the field of values, because that it is where corporate power and the state are vulnerable: the former because it often claims exemption from ethical criteria on the grounds of the absolute priority of the bottom line; the latter for the opposite reasons, that it has taken on the mantle of standing for society's collective values. Values are weak weapons in a conflict with money and power, but they are not meaningless. On occasions, the causes of the powerless can also deploy more substantive resources, such as demonstrations, strikes, boycotts, even disorder. Alternatively, as Charles Sabel and his colleagues have discussed (1999), civil society groups engage in practical schemes with local officials and regulators to raise standards in such fields as pollution control. But all these actions are usually rooted in a value-driven campaign.

We can consider at least five kinds of groups which are the quintessential actors in civil society, in large part driven by values.

First, we must consider the marginal case of political parties. These link the world of the state to the wider society, and are frequently the vehicles through which causes and issues enter the political system. They are therefore vital to civil society and essential channels for any attempt to contest corporate power within that system. They can however also become 'polluted channels', restricting flows of concerns to those which the leadership already wants to approve. In the early decades of democracy, and particularly among parties on the political left, there was a tendency among many people committed to public action to channel all such activity through a party and perhaps closely associated organizations. This was based in the belief that it was through the people pushing for power to the party-based, democratic state that the power of wealth could be challenged. The rest of society was seen as suffused by traditional and wealth-based power, against which the propertyless had this one weapon. Given the success of corporate power in capturing the state, this is today an unwise policy, if it ever did make sense. Parties that continue to follow it become the tools of state and corporation and thus the enemies of civil society. On the other hand, contemporary societies provide a mass of different, small power bases, that do not all ally with wealth. Individuals championing causes will be unwise if they limit their efforts to working through a party; they need to apply pressure at many points in a system. Parties in turn will be most effective channels for civil society when precisely the opposite strategy to the historic one is followed. They need to be open and welcoming to groups that wish to retain their autonomy but ally themselves to a party for some causes. This has been happening in most democracies for several years now, but it contends with party leaderships' counteracting need for obedience and order.

Second, religions may have lost their former sovereignty in the field of values, but they remain major participants in it, with resources autonomous of business and the state. They are vulnerable to capture by powerful economic interests – as has occurred in the USA with, for example, the role of churches in promulgating denial of the role of human causes of climate change. However, that is a hazard of all the groups being surveyed here. More important is the ability of religion to challenge the usually economically driven priorities of polity and economy alike and to present authoritatively supported ethical challenges, whether one agrees with them in individual cases or not.

Third are the campaigning groups already mentioned, the groups most likely to be thought of today when civil society is mentioned and specifically listed by Kocka, but in reality sharing that label with the others being considered here. Of course, campaigns do not necessarily counter the power of large corporations; one of the things the latter can do with their resources is to assist, or even create, campaigns that suit their interests. One poignant example are the groups that arise to champion the cause of medicines thought to provide an answer to cancers and other important illnesses, but about which health authorities are sceptical. Groups of patients and patients' families lobby for approval of the medicines. These seem classic cases of lively civil society, and often they are; but sometimes the campaign is led and funded by a pharmaceutical company hoping to rush authorities into premature approval of its drug.

Governments have been the main targets of civil society activities, for a rich diversity of causes ranging from opposition to torture to advancing the cause of wildlife. However, as discussed in the previous chapter, an increasingly important development in recent years has been the growth of campaigns aimed at corporations and seeking action directly from them rather than from government. It has been both a testament to the reality of the political power of the corporation and a challenge to it.

Fourth comes a category that overlaps with campaigning groups: the voluntary and charitable sector. We can distinguish between the two in that the former press governments, corporations and others to take action to address an identified problem, often in contestative and conflictual ways; voluntary organizations and charities engage in direct provision of resources to address the problem, using means other than those of state and firm. Many organizations combine both kinds of activity, but it is important here to give separate attention to voluntary organizations, to demonstrate that state and firm are not the only resource base in our societies. This was also noted in the case of churches, and there is considerable overlap in these categories too.

In its modern use the word 'charity' has strongly Christian origins, signifying Christian adaptation of the Latin *caritas*: the idea of universal love, both divine and human. It is a vastly more extensive term than the nineteenth-century concept of charity, but it can easily include that. It was developed to have this meaning by Thomas Aquinas in the thirteenth century, leading to a major renewal of interest in Aquinas's work six centuries later as European Catholics confronted the crises of poverty and social dislocation associated with the early years of the industrial revolution. Being universal in its scope, *caritas*, unlike other forms of love, can be directed towards strangers, and is altruistic, requiring no reciprocity. As such, it has long been used by the church to describe not only God's love but also the benevolent activities that it undertakes itself and which it commends to its followers. In the centuries before states accepted any welfare role, the distribution of welfare, part of the domain of the City of God, not of man, was the business of the church.

The contemporary concept of charitable activity descends directly and immediately from these ideas, but follows a particular logic. It is usually assumed that a publicly oriented activity can be understood in one (or more) of only three ways. It might rest in the polity, either as part of a drive for political power or as an activity mandated, funded and organized by the state; or it might rest in the market, either as part of a drive for private gain, or as an activity mandated, funded and organized by a firm. If it is neither of these, then it must rest in the realm of value, carried out for neither power nor material gain. It might, as with *caritas*, be carried out within the framework of a religious organization, but it might also be part of a fragmented set of secular organizations and informal groups.

In fact, charitable or voluntary activities are never found purely in the realm of value, but must share in the other realms: they employ staff and hold assets that require participation in the capitalist economy; they are regulated by laws that issue from the state; individuals working for charities may well have motives of private and personal advancement. All other organizations are similarly mixed: the state, too, uses the labour and property markets to carry out its activities, and calls on commitments of value and loyalty; firms need a legal base and try to generate loyalty among their employees. But charitable activities are distinguished by the value component playing a particularly large, indeed dominant, part. In this way they belong in the realm previously dominated by the church, even when fully secularized; and in societies where the state claims the dominant role in the definition of values, they represent a potential alternative, possibly even a rival.

What then is the legitimacy of charitable or voluntary activity? If it is rooted in a church, it claims the legitimacy of that faith. If it denotes a particular community of identity, it is claiming the legitimacy of that identity and the right or obligation of persons having that identity to do things for other members of it. Other claims assert the moral superiority of the truly universal. This is a difficult claim to make heard, but it is one towards which a good deal of charitable activity devotes itself. It involves constant discourse and dialogue, in which fragments of religious values, Kantian concepts of rational universalism and appeals to a sense of common human identity are all deployed. It is a discourse without hope of final resolution, agreement or resting place; but as it goes on, a good deal of practical activity takes place, governed in large part by the drive felt by very many people for a value-oriented (rather than politically or market-driven) means of connecting their individual private selves to an extensive sense of moral obligation somewhere 'out there'. In very recent decades, when risks of environmental damage have begun to threaten the planet itself and its climate, there has been a return to charitable concern for that most extensive entity of all: the natural world, taken for granted for so many centuries as civilization looked to an urban and social expression of itself.

Finally, I include within civil society the professions, by which I mean any occupational group which has developed a set of autonomously derived values about how it practises its activities, which may at times contest the logic of profit maximization. Some occupations have this formally built into their charters and training programmes. In other cases it may emerge in informal understandings among groups of workers. Like voluntary activity, professional work is not primarily set up to campaign and struggle; it is there to do a job, and its practitioners make money doing it. It is, however, rooted in values, and does on occasion provide scope for contesting the dominant logic of state and corporation.

Again, at least in the western world, these values ultimately derive from religion. The concepts of calling, vocation, the German *Beruf*, all derive from the idea of hearing a call from God to take up the religious life. The idea spread to certain secular occupations in the early modern period, keeping the aura of the religious idea that this is not simply a form of work, but a particular kind of work, to which the practitioner makes a moral commitment, to pursue beyond the extent of a private, material interest. The concept may become humbug in many individual cases, as it did within the church itself. Indeed, such moral claims may serve as a concealment and protection from suspicion, behind which even unscrupulous activities may be conducted. This is the interpretation of the professions that the managers of the marketized state are particularly keen to propose. However, the important point at the heart of the concept of the 'calling' is that work activity may acquire a public meaning via the realm of values, and not just because it is mandated by the state or a response to the market. Persons who pursue that concept of their role may come into conflict with the claims of the state and the firm, depending on who is engaging their services. The state will claim a democratic legitimacy to decide how and for what purpose work tasks should be conducted; the firm will claim that its board's or senior managers' interpretation of shareholders' interests must prevail over employees' sense of their own professional responsibilities. It can be difficult to avoid value struggles.

The claims of all these components of civil society – the autonomous political party, the church, the campaigning groups, the voluntary body, the profession – are potentially dangerous. Those who claim to act ethically can be pursuing personal ambition, and even acting corruptly, just as much as any business person or politician. Groups campaigning for causes will include those who define exclusive communities as well as those with an inclusive mission. Even those who stake their claim on universalism may be dangerous when they claim monopoly over interpretation of the universal (as the Catholic Church, the French Revolution, and the Soviet state all did in their turn). Professionals insisting on the arcane nature of their knowledge are in a position to fool the public or at least to engage in rent-seeking behaviour (extracting high fees) because customers cannot exercise intelligent market choice when, by definition, they do not share the knowledge that is needed to help them make a choice.

These organizations therefore need scrutiny and to be subject to criticism and monitoring as much as do firms and governments, and these latter bodies can reliably be expected to provide that, or at least towards those that have been critical of *them*. One thinks, for example, of the way in which scientists studying the impact of human action on climate change are harried by climate change denial groups funded by corporations. It is therefore important that critical and monitoring activities emerge out of civil society itself. What we do not want is for these various groups to come under the control of firms and governments. This sometimes happens, for example, when governments co-opt voluntary bodies into their own policy goals, offering them funding if they will follow the government agenda rather than their own, and using them to take over tasks normally associated with government itself.

There are no magic answers that will ensure that everyone working for civil society action sustains high moral purpose; nothing that will prevent corporations and states from interfering in civil society in order to generate activities favourable to their interests. All we can hope for is that there will be scope for diversity, and a constant supply of critical, questioning, quarrelsome voices and practical projects resulting from these. It may be difficult any longer to sustain an actual economy that is dominated by competition among masses of firms, rather than a Chicago market of giant corporations; but it is essential that civil society resembles that former kind of market.

Civil society seen in this way is an anarchic space; but this does not mean advocating overall anarchy, as states and corporations can be relied upon to keep us all in order. Civil society, as we have come to understand it today, operates in the interstices left among the great erections of political and economic power, like little houses springing up busily and untidily, creating vitality in a street dominated by the inaccessible security-controlled doors of skyscrapers. Since it contains a vast array of competing groups, with different and sometimes opposed moral agendas, it also embodies a kind of moral relativism. But this is moral relativism only at the meta-level of the character of the system as a whole. Within it the great majority of participants acts with moral purpose. In societies that contain a plurality of rival values, where no religion or set of beliefs has hegemony, that is all we can hope for.

8

What's Left of What's Right?

Neoliberalism came to prominence by triumphing over what had been – in some countries of the advanced world, but by no means all – 30 previous years of declining social and economic inequality and growing attention to social needs and collective goals, all primarily making use of the power of the democratic nation-state. Politically, the victory of neoliberalism seemed an historic defeat of the political centre-left, in terms of both ideas and organizational power; a victory of the right and its preference for strong, wealthy and powerful individuals against any ideas of extended collective interests going beyond those of the maintenance of order. By the mid-1990s there had been a response from parties from what had previously constituted the 'left', which took the form of accepting many of the tenets of neoliberalism while trying to sustain certain classic left-of-centre goals of strong public and social services. These were seen as necessary to compensate for the increased economic inequality accepted as being required by neoliberalism. This process started in the USA with Bill Clinton's 'New Democrats', spread to the United Kingdom as 'New Labour', less convincingly in Germany as 'die neue Mitte', and under the generic label of 'The Third Way' was welcomed with varying degrees of enthusiasm by formerly social democratic parties in the rest of western Europe and beyond. Many people were left bemused by the change: what was left of what they had become accustomed to think of as what was 'left': people wrote articles with phrases like 'What's left?' in the title.

This question has never been resolved. Meanwhile, the neoliberal model has now met its own crisis in the recent banking and finance debacle. Neoliberalism is wearing out, as all models do. It therefore becomes pertinent to ask: 'What is left of what is right?' The favoured doctrines of the contemporary political right now seem as tattered as those of the left had become by the 1980s. 'What is left of what is right?' can also be understood in two further meanings. The second asks what now stands to the left of the neoliberal right, given that the problem of 'what's left?' was never resolved by the 'third way' moment. The third meaning asks what is left to us for working out what values are right? Where can we get our bearings as to what constitute right actions in societies that have seen so much challenge to previous political certainties? In talking of right actions, I am assuming a place for ethics in human life, a place for some actions that consciously and willingly subordinate pursuit of self-interest to what we perceive to be a higher good, whether religious or humanist. Even if we remain primarily self-regarding, we have to face the fact that we can do little except when we are in some kind of relationship to other humans, or at least that other humans can do things to us. We therefore have an interest in the character of the various collectivities in which we find ourselves.

As was argued in Chapter 7, the dilemma between self and collectivity is not part of the conflict between market and polity. The political arena is at least as much dominated by personal interests as it is by moral concern; and economic philosophy has always insisted that the achievement of the market is to use individual striving to achieve collective welfare.

Very important progress was achieved on behalf of both the democratic polity and the mass market in a few limited

parts of the world and at various times from the late nineteenth to late twentieth centuries. It seems churlish to complain that both are currently being distorted in this heartland
– western Europe, North American, Australasia, Japan – at
a time when other parts of the world (in particular central
Europe, South Africa, India and some parts of Latin America)
are just beginning to enjoy some of their effects, albeit in a
halting way; and while the rest of the world has yet to taste
much of them at all. But problems in a heartland are particularly disturbing; and people in heartlands are prone to com-
placency and failure to see that the institutions of which they
boast are losing their grip. Both the democratic polity and
the market are experiencing deficits at the present time, deficits which link together at certain worrying points.

Democracy's problem is that mass publics are too remote
and too disaggregated to ensure that politicians are under
appropriate detailed constraint, certainly compared with
that exercised by corporate power. The two main mechanisms that act as intermediaries between public and political
elites – parties and the mass media – are becoming unfit for
purpose. Political parties are losing their links with movements of opinion emerging from the mass of the people,
leading them to seek extensive funds to generate synthetic
links between themselves and that public. The only major
sources of large funds are corporations and extremely
wealthy individuals. The mass media, fundamental to the
functioning of democracy, are increasingly the creatures of
giant corporations and extremely wealthy individuals. Corporate interests and wealthy individuals dominate democratic processes, and have rather particular interests of their
own. The purest expression of this kind of politics to date
is the set of leading media outlets, financial and other corporations and a political party around the persona of Silvio
Berlusconi, the prime minister and richest man of Italy at
the time of writing. But in other parts of the world too,
where democracy is being newly created, a major role is
played by parties that are emerging, not from deeply rooted
movements of opinion, but from very wealthy individuals,

The party then becomes their vehicle for advancing simultaneously their political and corporate ambitions.

Such phenomena become a problem for the market, not just for democracy. There is no political or economic theory that can demonstrate how giant corporations, relatively free from constraints of the market, or capable of dominating them, and increasingly becoming the main sources of power over politics, can be trusted with our collective goals. Chicago economics and its consumer welfare thesis try to do this, not convincingly, at the level of the economy, but cannot at all tackle the political implications of the monopoly-ridden, politicized economy that it legitimates. They here show themselves to be defective in relation to earlier traditions of market liberal thought. Classic liberalism set an economy of many competing firms within a polity of many competing interests, and with strict limits on the intertwining of economic and political power. German *Ordoliberalismus* envisaged free markets embedded in a legal system guaranteeing the survival of a property-owning middle class that would in turn prevent the political dominance of big capital and big labour, and was equally concerned to prevent concentrations of combined political and economic power. But these earlier schools of economic liberalism do not realistically describe today's economy; Chicago, for all its defects, does do that.

While globalization has seen a vast increase in competition and gains for consumers in many product markets, it has also produced some sectors where the need for firms to have adequate size to operate across the world at large has produced high entry barriers, favouring a small number of giant corporations, benefiting in particular from network externalities. There is, as a result, a growing inequality within and between nations, seen in the emergence of some individuals and corporations with very high concentrations of wealth. US firms are at the forefront of these developments, because several aspects of US society, including the state and its military apparatus, themselves constitute network externalities that favour US firms. Not surprisingly,

US economists, and business and political leaders are eager to spread support around the world for this kind of economy, a project for which they have been able to use that country's overwhelming influence on international organizations like the IMF and the OECD. That these ideas, which depend so much on US state power for their dominance, are supposed to stress the autonomy of the economy from the state is a particularly rich irony.

The ideological triumph of neoliberalism has led to too much reliance being placed on the bundles of quasi-market and corporate forces that constitute the economy. No problems are seen in these dominating polity, the world of values and the rest of society. In several countries we have seen this in a privatization process that has done little more than deliver monopoly public utilities into the hands of politically connected private owners – the very process that was criticized so strongly by the original eighteenth-century proponents of free markets. On a different scale, the effective privatization of demand management, discussed in Chapter 5, produced a global financial crisis and an extraordinary bout of irresponsible behaviour, not by a murky semi-criminal fringe of firms, but by the world's leading banks and other financial institutions. Within a pure market, efficiency and, therefore, the overall wealth of society are both maximized when profits are maximized. A firm that is running at a loss is wasting scarce resources and hurting us all. However, as we have seen in our discussions of externalities, public goods and merit goods, some desirable things are not covered by firms' profit-making activities and may even be damaged by them and by the extension of their logic into other areas of life.

Governments are usually seen, correctly, as the only organizations powerful and 'public' enough to be able to impose any different criteria of judgement, if the creation of wealth through economic efficiency is deemed to be morally inadequate or to prevent the achievement of other goods. However, governments are also aware that the resources they need to pursue any such goods are dependent on the creation of wealth, and corporations are seen as the single most reliable structures for creating wealth and for declaring the public policies that are needed for that task. The pursuit of profit by firms therefore enjoys an overwhelming privilege as a social goal, even for the achievement of objectives that cannot be achieved directly by profit maximization itself.

It is untrue that firms are the sole sources of wealth creation: education, publicly funded research, roads and other infrastructures, the systems of civil and criminal justice, and several other non-marketable collective and public goods contribute importantly to the process. Indeed, everyone pays lip service to that idea. However, when it comes to hard reasoning, wealth is only measurable when it appears in the profit accounts of corporations. For example, all profits made by Internet gambling firms automatically contribute to wealth creation and therefore, it seems, to human welfare; as a result, they are beyond reproach. Medical research can only prove its worth when a corporation succeeds in turning its work into clearly effective cures – or, into medicines that can be traded commercially. It will be the Internet gambling billionaire, not the medical researcher who plays her part in finding a new cancer treatment (unless she sets herself up as a highly prosperous company), who will have the capacity to own newspapers and sports clubs, to advise governments, to be invited on to the governing boards and privileged sponsors' lists of cultural establishments, to influence the policies of a political party – because Internet gambling produces money, and money talks.

As we have seen, the state and its institutions have been criticized from the same neoliberal perspective for not being more like firms. Indeed, one of the main achievements of the neoliberal political project is to place more or less all institutions in society – universities, hospitals, charities as well as governments – under an obligation to behave as though they were business corporations. They are doomed to fail this test. By definition, if efficiency is optimally defined as organizing all activities around a single goal of profit maximization, any organization that has multiple goals is suspected of inefficiency. But democracy is often effective enough to ensure that public service organizations do have multiple goals.

In an attempt to find alternatives to the state and enable it to 'shrink' as neoliberals require, increasing expectations are placed on charitable cause organizations, the voluntary sector. At the time of writing, the main manifestation of this is the so-called 'Big Society' programme of the Conservative–Liberal Democrat coalition government in the UK, where volunteers are being called on not to supplement public service activities, as they have usually done, but to replace them. But these voluntary organizations increasingly have to apply to wealthy individuals and corporations for financial help. There has often been a generous response to these appeals, but of course the wealthy express their personal preferences when deciding what causes they will support. This enables them to use their private wealth to make public decisions. Governments have sought to encourage this private giving, as it reduces the pressure on themselves to help support the causes. They do this by allowing tax remission on money used to make charitable donations, reinforcing the amount of the gift by the amount of taxation remitted. This therefore increases the wealthy individual's effect on public policy, as he/she is able to affect the destination of public funds in the form of the taxation foregone. Further, governments want to encourage charitable causes to be more active in seeking donations, in order further to reduce their own burden; they therefore inform charities that government funding will go disproportionately to those who have successfully raised money from the private sector – extending further the ability of wealthy individuals to determine the allocation of public funds.

Finally, in a further attempt to bring private sector efficiencies to the public sector, governments tend to appoint individuals who have acquired corporate wealth and risen to powerful positions within corporations to preside over public bodies, enabling these persons to extend their public policy reach even further. At every point we find that democratic market societies under the influence of neoliberal ideas throw more and more power, influence and privilege at the extremely wealthy, especially the wielders of large corporate resources.

There is a widely accepted view that inequality does not matter provided nearly everyone (within the boundaries of a particular nation-state) is reasonably well off. Provided everyone has a sound and warm house to live in, does it matter if some people have vast estates and luxury yachts? Their yachts do not diminish our houses. But this misses the point about inequality of wealth: It leads to inequalities of power that reach out from one arena of society into many others in a concentrated, centralizing way. The capacity of some individuals and families always to get their own way, to make the world according to their preferences rather than those of others, and to concentrate the privileges of many spheres of life upon themselves, does diminish the lives of others. The rest of us are all losers, as the scope for our exercise of choice outside that of goods presented to us in the market, our chance to create some little corners of life where non-commercial criteria might survive, are diminished. This is not what Adam Smith, Thomas Jefferson or the German *Ordoliberalen* believed would be brought to us by the market economy.

As we discussed in Chapter 6, this universal corporate dominance then has some paradoxical consequences for the corporation itself. Far too obviously and publicly prominent, giant corporations are less and less able to escape with the argument that they just exist in the market and cannot be expected to take account of anything wider than their immediate financial interests. Whether they like it or not, whether it can be justified by economic theory or not, firms are increasingly being seen as politically and socially responsible actors. There is a whole new politics around corporations, as campaigners expose their undesirable actions and try to influence customers and sometimes investors and employees. This can, given the right pressures from activists and regulators, turn corporate social responsibility from being an aspect of corporate public relations to a sharp and penetrating demand for corporate social accountability.

There is growing recognition among political scientists that both firms and the campaigns that criticize them now form part of the global polity, as recent articles by Pierre-Yves Néron (2010) and David Vogel (2008), cited in Chapter 6, show.

Ironically, this becomes in turn yet another means by which corporations become the dominant organizations in society. It is through their internal, undemocratic and non-transparent decision-making procedure that some causes are adopted and publicized, others ignored. In so many different ways, all routes through the neoliberal agenda, including attempts to oppose it, lead not to the market as such, but to the corporation.

Back to the State?

The financial crisis did produce one solid check to the case for a diminishing role for the state, in that deregulation of the financial sector was very widely agreed to have gone too far. The belief in the virtues of freeing capitalist activity from as much regulation as possible, absolutely central to neoliberal strategy, had excellent opportunities to realize itself from the 1980s to the 2000s. The financial crisis more or less tested it to destruction, and even some neoliberals now concede a need for some regulation, even though they continue to clamour for a 'shrinking state' elsewhere – and one can confidently expect demands for re-deregulation of banking once it can be assumed that most people have forgotten what caused the crisis. (Demands for a 'shrinking state' are in any case usually targeted at only certain state activities – those associated with the democratic state as a provider of services and security to the mass of the population. Neoliberals rarely call for a roll-back of those state activities that hearken back to an earlier pre-democratic age when governments served the interests of elites only: the extension of official honours and symbolic privileges to the rich and powerful; the establishment of an elaborate apparatus of law, prisons and police forces to protect private property and guarantee its rights; the awarding of lucrative public contracts.)

Looking at the other side of the coin, however, it is remarkable how much government activity has survived over three decades of neoliberal dominance. Collective and public goods that the market and corporations cannot provide can easily be neglected and fall into disrepair by the shrinking state, but the risks of ignoring them altogether have had to be heeded by the most neoliberal regimes. To take just four examples: public education, the maintenance of roads, the regulation of privatized but monopoly utilities, some protection against environmental damage: all remain the object of some kind of major political debate and government action in all democracies. And it is democracy, inadequate though it may be, and not the overall size of the state, that ensures that neoliberals will always have to make some compromises with a collective and public agenda. The appalling record of environmental damage and neglect of infrastructure of undemocratic state socialism demonstrated clearly to us that an extensive state without democracy guarantees nothing in the pursuit of collective goods.

Debates about what states should or should not do go on in a lively fashion in much political debate. I want here to turn the attention of critics of neoliberalism in a different direction. While it is necessary to rebut the wilder attacks on the need for governments to be part of the solutions we seek to many problems, it is also necessary for people on the centre-left to move away from the virtual identification of the pursuit of the collective with assertion of the power of the centralized state that has dominated their thinking since the French Revolution. There are arguments for this that are quite different from those that would be used by neoliberals, several of which have appeared at various points in preceding chapters.

First, since it is impossible to envisage an economy that is not dominated by giant firms and in which they are unable to translate economic power into political influence, governments cannot be trusted not to be exceptionally responsive to these firms' interests. This means that all use of the state as a check on or regulator of corporate power will be, at best, a matter of 'two steps forward, one step back'.

Second, the state is not a force with necessarily clean hands, but is itself an area within which individuals seek personal advantage and aggrandisement. True, it is likely to be more free from such vices than are corporations. The actions and decision-making processes of governments are far more subject to transparency rules and open procedures than firms, which are able to use arguments about commercial confidentiality to justify high levels of secrecy in their operations. Exercises of nepotism and favouritism that attract strong criticism in the political sphere pass as normal behaviour in business. Politics at least has to pay lip service to relating to a world of values and some idea of right conduct, while firms are able to argue – though with increasing difficulty – that all they need do is make money. In fact, they do not need to 'argue' at all, as firms are not required to come to any arena of public debate, whereas politicians in a democracy can never escape it. However, while in general the world of politics is under greater pressure than that of business to respect values, it remains one in which active individuals' primary motivation will usually be their personal advancement. While this is subject to democratic check, that is a rather blunt instrument – sometimes blunter than the constraints imposed by the market on corporate behaviour.

Furthermore, any superiority of moral stance by the state in relation to business is among those many characteristics of the democratic polity that is being eroded as the state responds to pressures to learn more from business. Several examples have been given in previous chapters, but a further one can be considered here. Considerable attention has been paid in recent years to the concept of 'nudge', the title of a book by two American academics, economist Richard Thaler and lawyer Cass Sunstein (2008). They describe – with approval – the techniques used by firms gently to lure customers into making purchases without realizing what they are doing, and suggest ways in which governments and others might use the same techniques to encourage people to make, for example, healthy lifestyle choices. Interestingly, politicians of many parties have seized on this idea as a way in which governments might affect citizens' behaviour without making laws and regulations to coerce them and without interfering with their actual capacity to choose. Sunstein has become an official in President Obama's centre-left administration, and great admiration has been expressed by the idea of 'nudge' by the British right-of-centre Conservative Party.

At the heart of the concept is the fact that citizens/customers are lured into doing things without their being aware that this is happening to them – though if they do spot it the 'nudger' is powerless to prevent it. To do something to people without their being aware is to take advantage of their lack of knowledge or information. It is incompatible with both democratic and market principles; but it is of the essence of modern corporate behaviour. The more an economy is dominated by giant firms, the more this asymmetry develops between them and citizen-consumers. And the more politics follows this business example, the worse grows the asymmetry between governments and citizens. Thaler and Sunstein proceeded from admirable motives: if various psychological tricks are used to persuade people to buy things, would it not be better to use them to persuade people to be good citizens or look after their own health? But once politicians get to work on such an idea, its sinister side emerges, as transparency about what government is doing diminishes.

A third and rather different reason for not seeing the resurgence of the state as a simple strategy for reform is that political power remains overwhelmingly tied to the level of the nation-state. Not only does this mean that it has problems acting as a truly 'public' force on the global stage, but political parties and governments continue to try to define interests in national terms. In an increasingly global economy this is not only unrealistic, but it encourages an irrational nationalism. From here it is an easy slip to the defence of the public realm becoming the defence of a particular national population against 'foreigners', especially immigrants and ethnic minorities. As formal competition among the main established parties in many countries becomes drained of content – partly because all parties are essentially following a corporate agenda – xenophobic movements emerge as the only sources of real choice and novelty. And all they are doing is taking to an extreme the exaltation of competitive national identity being used by nearly all shades of political opinion.

In this context transnational corporations (TNCs) appear as refreshingly cosmopolitan forces, responding flexibly to the post-national geography appropriate to a globalized economy. If asserting the democratic state against global corporations becomes a matter of nationalistic protection, it will be a backward step. As we know from past protectionist periods, the consequences are not only shrinking trade and overall declines in wealth, but also an increase in tension and hostility between people from different ethnic and national backgrounds. But what are we to do when the assertion of national citizenship rights becomes our only defence against the power of TNCs to disrupt our lives? There are particularly important issues here in labour law, where the protection of employee rights against TNCs playing off groups of workers in wealthier countries against those in countries with low wages and bad working conditions can only be waged at national level.

Beyond State, Market and Corporation

I am assuming that anyone reading this book is interested in the idea of public life as an arena for expressing and realizing values, even if we might disagree over what those values might be. Certainly, anyone primarily interested in either politics or business solely as mechanisms for personal advancement and enrichment will have stopped reading long before this point. The previous chapter traced in a highly schematic way the frequently unhappy history of how values fit into human institutions, at least in western societies. Organized religions have been very unworthy of their special claims to be the guardians of values. Firms have a very fleeting relationship to values, despite occasional flourishes of philanthropy and CSR. The polity still appears as the main forum where value questions are debated and where values are expected to be collectively pursued in modern societies; but I have been arguing against our ability to take that for granted. Where then can the pursuit of values be located? Where do we find well springs of moral seriousness in what is otherwise just a game of power play among different organizations and, in particular, their leaders?

The previous chapter led us to look for answers to the inchoate mass of forces generally known as civil society, not because its organizations can in themselves be trusted any more than any other institutions managed by human beings, but because of its capacity to generate a genuine pluralism. Civil society will be stronger, the more that the state and the giant firm are challenged – by churches, voluntary organizations, professions and other participants in the fragmented world of values – and required to participate in a pluralist dialogue that escapes their control.

The previous chapter discussed the idea of professional ethics as a form of institutionalization of values. This is a highly unfashionable claim to make at the present time, as there is a widespread consensus in firms and governments alike that professionals are not to be trusted but must be brought under the control of managers who will set them performance targets to replace their unreliable ethic. These managers, it is claimed, are in turn subject to the market, which guarantees their own behaviour. The first major occupation to pass from governance by professional standards to those of the market was tabloid journalism. Journalists liberated from commercial criteria would probably behave more like academics and teachers, which one can take to mean, as one chooses, guided either by a professional ethic of commitment to a search for objective knowledge or by the self-indulgence of personal curiosity. One is free to carry out a thought experiment: would the world be improved if teachers and doctors conducted their professions in the manner of tabloid journalists, or vice versa?

As professions of all kinds come under increasing pressure to conform to commercial criteria, the former alternative is more likely to happen. Professional ethics would then affect behaviour only if users of the professions can make a demand for ethical behaviour effective through market choices – which to some extent of course they will try to do. It is good and important that we assert standards of professional ethics and require the professions to substantiate their claims. The more occupations that we could subject to such standards, the more trust we could all have in each other. But the dominant tendencies in both states and firms are in the opposite direction: to ridicule the idea of professional ethics, to seek less rather than more reliance on a demand for it, and to encourage us to place more reliance on market processes that are themselves highly vulnerable to manipulation by public and private managements alike. The point is that we cannot risk relying on any one mechanism to ensure that each other's behaviour is guided by ethical standards. As John Kay has observed (2007), we certainly cannot write off the role that personal professional commitment offers to insert some ethical quality in society's decision making, as some interpretations of new public management and the principal–agent model would have us do. We need strong civil societies in which a diversity of kinds of pressure is able to flourish, so that we can then compare and criticize.

These arguments about civil society are not new. Back in the 1950s the late US economist J. K. Galbraith (1952) wrote of the need for groups of 'employees, consumers, savers and shareholders' to exert a balancing power against corporate might. In the late 1990s Giuliano Amato (1997) ended his study of antitrust law by explicitly recalling Galbraith's words and commending them to our own day. Slightly later the British political scientist David Marquand (2004) wrote of the 'need to redress the balance between the commercial invasion of government and a top-down state by reasserting civic muscle', through the moral commitments of an engaged citizenry. It is a remarkable fact that all three of these men have been political insiders, at different periods and in different countries. Galbraith was a central member of the group around the US presidency of J. F. Kennedy in the early 1960s; Amato has in recent years held the posts of prime minister and other senior offices in the Italian state; Marquand was a British member of parliament in the 1970s and subsequently played an important role in the European Commission. Yet none of them suggests that we try to resolve the issues at stake through the formal political process. They direct us to that wider world of civil society.

This is both bad and good news. It is bad, because it amounts to pitting against the might of both corporate and government institutions the 'power of the powerless'. Also, in the end much civil action has to find a response at the level of government if it is to get anywhere. This is the sobering message of a book by Debra Spini (2006) on post-national civil society (*La società postnazionale*). Having opened up to us an exciting vista of citizens' actions extending across national boundaries, she reminds us of the continued presence of the indispensible gatekeeper, the solidly national democratic state. And the political party, manipulated though that institution has become, remains a major gatekeeper en route to that primary gatekeeper.

But the news is good, because it shows us that there are things that ordinary citizens can do. I said in the Preface that this book is directed at those who have to cope with the world rather than those who try radically to reshape it. But coping can include campaigning successfully for many minor victories. Governments do often intervene to protect citizens from corporate abuse, as official campaigns against smoking and unhealthy foods, which have, if anything, been strengthened in recent years, demonstrate. Such cases give us hope. These government actions can usually be traced back to small groups of poorly funded but passionately committed professionals and people of good will. Firms that boast of their green or fair trade credentials did not dream up these ideas in their marketing departments; they were responding to serious customer pressure, which was in turn responding to campaigning by small numbers of concerned activists in ecological groups and trade unions. There is no need for defeatism. Rarely before in human history has there been so little deference shown to authority, so much demand for openness, so many cause organizations, journalists and academics devoting themselves to criticizing those who hold power and holding up their actions to scrutiny. New electronic forms of communication are enabling more and more causes to express themselves in highly public ways.

Also, to examine the other side of Spini's coin: a good deal of civil society action crosses national boundaries in a way that political parties find so difficult. Many cause groups have become truly post-national in their membership, leadership and focus. Paradoxically, TNCs themselves help construct a post-national civil society. By themselves operating across the globe, they enable campaigning groups to recognize some shared interests that they would rarely discover if they limited themselves to formal politics and its national confines.

Finally, civil society action can embrace the political role of the corporation in a way that political parties, even where they have not become dependent on corporate funds, have little incentive to do. The main incentive for a political party in an electoral democracy is to turn blame on to rival parties. If firms misbehave, there are few rewards for an opposition party in criticizing them; better to blame the government for not having controlled the firms' behaviour. Corporate perpetrators slink away out of the spotlight. A good deal of that happened during the financial crisis. There were even attempts to blame President Obama for the Gulf of Mexico oil disaster, even though he had a record of being critical of off-shore oil drilling, while his opponents supported it.

If, as we have seen above, firms are active and powerful in shaping the rules of the market and the general political framework within which they operate, this party politicization becomes totally inadequate. Civil society campaigning groups do not have the same incentive as parties to turn all criticism towards government alone, and in this way too are in a better position than political parties to shape debate appropriate to our times. Of course, cause movements can themselves be corrupted. On the one hand, they are tempted to exaggerate their case to attract publicity. On the other, in desperate need for resources as they always are, they are easily compromised by political or corporate blandishments, whether for the sake of their organizational funds or the individual careers of their leaders. Fighting for causes is tough, unremitting work. It goes on unceasing, with permanent watchfulness, never able to say: 'We have achieved our goals; we can rest now.'

So, what is left of what is right? In the first sense of this sentence, what remains of neoliberalism after the financial crisis, the answer must be 'virtually everything'. The combination of economic and political forces behind this agenda is too powerful for it to be fundamentally dislodged from its predominance. Already we have seen how a crisis caused by appalling behaviour among banks has been redefined as a crisis of public spending. Bankers' bonuses are returning to their pre-crisis level, while thousands of public employees are losing their jobs.

To the second sense, 'what now constitutes a viable left opposition to neoliberalism?', the answer is more complex. The arguments in this book give no support to a resumed search for a state-dominated economy, but one in which there is continued, enduring tension among a quadrilateral of forces, each of which is needed to make a good society: state, market, corporation, civil society. Provided this tension is creative, it can deliver both entrepreneurial innovation and restraints on inequalities of power, though it is likely to proceed under the shadow of continued dominance by corporate wealth.

The final sense – what remains of our search for values, an understanding of what constitutes the right things to do – also delivers an essentially liberal answer. In our normatively fragmented societies values can only emerge from dispute and struggle. We can however go beyond that and point to the need for values to embrace collective and public goals. The values of individualism as such, and of rights in the sense of the right to be left alone are cop-outs. We are unable to sustain our lives by ourselves and we run a considerable risk that the way we conduct our lives can damage those of others. We cannot own property or engage in the market without reliance that others will accept our ownership claims and defend them. We are enmeshed in needs for collective and public goods. To seek to wriggle out from the challenges that this presents is to wriggle out of being human.

References

Amato, G. 1997. *Antitrust and the Bounds of Power*. Oxford: Hart.

Bork, R. H. 1993. *The Antitrust Paradox: A Policy at War with Itself*. 2nd edn. New York: Free Press. (Originally 1978)

Buchanan, J. M. and Tullock, G. 1962. *The Calculus of Consent*. Ann Arbor: University of Michigan Press.

Campbell, J. 2007. Why Would Corporations Behave in Socially Responsible Ways? An Institutional Theory of Corporate Social Responsibility. *Academy of Management Review*, 32, 3: 946–67.

Coase, R. 1937. The Nature of the Firm. *Economica*, 4: 386–405.

Coase, R. 1960. The Problem of Social Cost. *Journal of Law and Economics*, 3: 1–44.

Crane, A., Matten, D. and Moon, J. 2008. *Corporations and Citizenship*. Cambridge: Cambridge University Press.

Cucinotta, A., Pardolesi, R. and Van Den Bergh, R. (eds) 2002. *Post-Chicago Developments in Antitrust Law*. Cheltenham: Elgar.

Dahl, R. A. 1982. *Dilemmas of Pluralist Democracy: Autonomy Versus Control*. New Haven, CT: Yale University Press.

Friedman, M. 1970. The Social Responsibility of Business Is to Increase its Profits. *New York Times Magazine*, 13 September.

Friedman, M. and Friedman, R. D. 1980. *Free to Choose*. New York: Harcourt.

Froud, J., Johal, S., Papazian, V. and Williams, K. 2004. The Temptation of Houston: A Case Study of Financialisation. *Critical Perspectives On Accounting*, 15, 6–7: 885–909.

Galbraith, J. K. 1952. *American Capitalism: The Concept of Counter-Vailing Power.* Boston: Houghton-Mifflin.

Green, D. and Shapiro, I. 1996. *Pathologies of Rational Choice Theory.* New Haven, CT: Yale University Press.

Havel, V. 1985. *The Power of the Powerless.* London: Hutchinson.

Hertz, N. 2001. Better to Shop than Vote? *Business Ethics: A European Review*, 10: 190–3.

Hirschman, A. 1977. *The Passions and the Interests: Political Arguments for Capitalism Before Its Triumph.* Princeton, NJ: Princeton University Press.

IMF 2010. *A Fistful of Dollars: Lobbying and the Financial Crisis.* Washington, DC: International Monetary Fund.

Jensen, M. 2001. Value Maximization, Stakeholder Theory, and the Corporate Objective Function. *Journal of Applied Corporate Finance*, 14, 3: 8–21.

Johnson, S. 2009. The Quiet Coup. *Atlantic Home*, May.

Kay, J. 2007. The Failure of Market Failure. *Prospect*, 26 July.

Kocka, J. 2004. Civil society in Historical Perspective. *European Review*, 12, 1: 65–79.

Le Grand, J. 2006. *Motivation, Agency and Public Policy: Of Knights and Knaves, Pawns and Queens.* Revised paperback edn. Oxford: Oxford University Press.

Lindblom, C. E. 1977. *Politics and Markets.* New York: Basic Books.

Marquand, D. 2004. *The Decline of the Public: The Hollowing Out of Citizenship.* Cambridge: Cambridge University Press.

Néron, P.-Y. 2010. Business and the Polis: What Does it Mean to See Corporations as Political Actors? *Journal of Business Ethics*, 94, 3: 333–52.

OECD 1994. *The Jobs Study.* Paris: OECD.

Olson, M. 1982. *The Rise and Decline of Nations.* New Haven: Yale University Press.

Posner, R. A. 2001. *Antitrust Law.* 2nd edn. Chicago: University of Chicago Press.

Rasche, A. and Kell, G. 2010. *The UN Global Compact: Achievements, Trends and Challenges.* Cambridge: Cambridge University Press.

Reich, R. 2008. *Supercapitalism.* New York: Vintage Books.

Roy, W. G. 1997. *Socializing Capital: The Rise of the Large Industrial Corporation in America*. Princeton, NY: Princeton University Press.

Ruggie, J. G. 2007. Business and Human Rights: The Evolving International Agenda. *American Journal of International Law*, 101, 4: 819–40.

Ruggie, J. G. 2009. Business and Human Rights: Towards Operationalizing the 'Protect, Respect and Remedy' Framework. United Nations Human Rights Council, Eleventh Session, New York, 22 April.

Sabel, C., Fung, A. and Karkainen, B. 1999. Beyond Backyard Environmentalism. *Boston Review*, 24, 5.

Schmalensee, R. 2002. *Lessons from the Microsoft Case*. Florence: European University Institute.

Spini, D. 2006. *La società postnazionale*. Rome: Meltemi.

UK Treasury 2004. *Microeconomic Reform in Britain: Delivering Opportunities for All*. London: HMSO.

Vogel, D. 2008. Private Global Business Regulation. *Annual Review of Political Science*, 11: 261–82.

Williamson, O. E. 1975. *Markets and Hierarchies: Analysis and Antitrust Implications: A Study in the Economics of Internal Organization*. New York: Free Press.

Williamson, O. E. 1985. *The Economic Institutions of Capitalism*. New York: Free Press.

Williamson, O. E. and Masten, S. E. 1995. *Transaction Cost Economics*. Aldershot: Edward Elgar.

Wolf, M. 2008. *Fixing Global Finance*. Baltimore, MD: Johns Hopkins University Press.

Further Reading

Chapter 1 The Previous Career of Neoliberalism

Amato, G. 1997. *Antitrust and the Bounds of Power*. Oxford: Hart.

Campbell, J. L. and Pedersen, O. K. (eds) 2001. *The Rise of Neoliberalism and Institutional Analysis*. Princeton, NJ: Princeton University Press.

Harvey, D. 2005. *A Brief History of Neoliberalism*. Oxford: Oxford University Press.

Medema, S. G. 2009. *The Hesitant Hand: Taming Self Interest in the History of Economic Ideas*. Princeton, NJ: Princeton University Press.

Chapter 4 Private Firms and Public Business

Flinders, M. 2005. The Politics of Public–Private Partnerships, *British Journal of Politics and International Relations*, 7: 215–39.

Freedland, M. 1998. Public Law and Private Finance – Placing the Private Finance Initiative in a Public Frame. *Public Law*: 288–307.

Froud, J. and Shaoul, J. 2001. Appraising and Evaluating PFI for NHS Hospitals. *Financial Accountability and Management*, 17, 3: 247–70.

Osborne, D. and Gaebler, T. (1992). *Reinventing Government: How the Entrepreneurial Spirit Is Transforming the Public Sector.* Wokingham: Addison-Wesley.

Chapter 5 Privatized Keynesianism: Debt in Place of Discipline

Bellofiore, R. and Halevi, J. Forthcoming. Deconstructing Labor: A Marxian-Kaleckian Perspective on What Is 'New' in Contemporary Capitalism and Economics. In C. Gnos and L.-P. Rochon (eds), *Employment, Growth and Development: A Post-Keynesian Approach*, Cheltenham: Elgar.

Boyer, R. 2005. From Shareholder Value to CEO Power: The Paradox of the 1990s. *Competition & Change*, 9, 1: 7–47.

Davis, G. F. 2009. *Managed by the Markets: How Finance Reshaped America.* Oxford: Oxford University Press.

Finlayson, A. 2009. Financialisation, Financial Literacy and Asset-Based Welfare. *British Journal of Politics & International Relations*, 11, 3: 400–21.

Hay, C. 2009. Good Inflation, Bad Inflation: The Housing Boom, Economic Growth and the Disaggregation of Inflationary Preferences in the UK and Ireland. *British Journal of Politics & International Relations*, 11, 3: 461–78.

Kay, J. 2009. *The Long and the Short of It.* London: The Erasmus Press.

Chapter 6 From Corporate Political Entanglement To Corporate Social Responsibility

Mellahi, K., Morrell, K. and Wood, G. 2010. *The Ethical Business.* London: Palgrave.

Chapter 7 Values and Civil Society

Hallberg, P. and Wittrock, B. 2006. From *koinonia politikè* to *societas civilis*: Birth, Disappearance and First Renaissance of the Concept. In P. Wagner (ed.), *The Languages of Civil Society*. Oxford: Berghahn.

Keane, J. (ed.) 2006. *Civil Society: Berlin Perspectives*. Oxford: Berghahn.

Van Kersbergen, K. 1995. *Social Capitalism: A Study of Christian Democracy and the Welfare State*. London: Routledge.

Index

regulatory capture 72
Reich, Robert 66
Reid, John 93
religions
  charitable sector 156, 157,
    158
  in civil society 153, 155
  collectivism and
    individualism 145, 146,
    148
  state power, reliance on
    148–9
  value component 148, 150,
    155, 157–8, 175
  vulnerability to economic
    interests 155
rent-seeking behaviour 129
risk
  buying and selling 97
  calculable 97
  optimistic trading 101
  ratings agencies 100
  secondary markets in 98,
    99–103, 106, 110, 116,
    117, 120, 123
  sensitivity to 59
  short-term calculations 99,
    102
risk-sharing 102, 110
road tolls 38
Ruggie, John 137–8
Russian Revolution 8

Sarbanes-Oxley Act 120
Schmalensee, Richard 69
Second World War 12
secondary markets 44–5, 116,
    123
  asset bundles 99, 110,
    117
  collapse of 117

  in ethical corporate
    behaviour 140
  and the financial crisis 110,
    117, 123
  re-establishment 120
  velocity of transactions 99,
    102, 106, 124
share markets
  and innovation 102
  secondary market's
    distortion of 116–17
shareholder maximization
  concept of the firm 44,
    57, 58, 62, 63, 91, 103–9,
    136, 139
shareholders
  capacity to be moral agents
    105–6
  conflicts of interest 108
  earnings 106
  losses, compensation for 107
  shift in the role of
    shareholding 106–8
  transfer of risk away from
    109
'shrinking state', demands for
    170
Singapore, neoliberal regime 21
social democracy 8–13, 27,
    76, 116, 119
  goals and policies 9, 10
  moderate centre-left politics
    9
  political parties and
    mindsets 9
  principal tenets 13
  social compromises 9–10
  social experiment, failure of
    14
  Third Way Social
    Democrats 27